IMAGES
of America

REYNOLDA
1906–1924

By the 1910s, the desire to live in a bungalow had become so pervasive that wealthy clients asked architects to design the one-and-a-half-story house on a large scale. Philadelphia architect Charles Barton Keen met the challenge of designing Reynolda, shown above, by adding lateral wings to a bungalow-style central block. Then he disguised its height by running a sunken-roof deck between the chimneys. From wing to wing, the house measures 255 feet in length. (Reynolda House Museum of American Art Archives.)

ON THE COVER: This aerial view shows Reynolda's original entrance drive and forecourt. The wide, sweeping front lawn converts to a nine-hole golf course, affording an uninterrupted view from the bungalow of nearly a half-mile. The rear vista looks down a tree-framed slope to a newly built lake that spreads across 16 acres. In the background, the road to the left leads to the village, and the road to the right leads to outlying fields. (Reynolda House Museum of American Art Archives.)

IMAGES
of America

REYNOLDA
1906–1924

Barbara Babcock Millhouse

ARCADIA
PUBLISHING

Published by Arcadia Publishing
Charleston, South Carolina

Library of Congress Control Number: 2010937377

For all general information, please contact Arcadia Publishing:
Telephone 843-853-2070
Fax 843-853-0044
E-mail sales@arcadiapublishing.com
For customer service and orders:
Toll-Free 1-888-313-2665

Visit us on the Internet at www.arcadiapublishing.com

Dedicated to my grandchildren Zachary, Grace, Natalie, Rebecca, Sarah, and Charlotte, so they will know that dreams can come true.

Katharine Smith Reynolds is shown here in 1921. (Reynolda House Museum of American Art Archives.)

CONTENTS

Acknowledgments		6
Introduction		7
Photograph Legend		8
1.	Meeting the Reynolds Family	9
2.	Building Reynolda	21
3.	Bungalow Grounds	35
4.	Lake and Boathouse	49
5.	Greenhouses and Formal Gardens	63
6.	Village East of Reynolda Road	77
7.	Village West of Reynolda Road	97
8.	Five Row	111
9.	Garden Parties, Polo, and Memorials	119

ACKNOWLEDGMENTS

My gratitude goes out to Sherry Hollingsworth, without whom writing this book would not have been possible. She coordinated the project at every stage. Her background in landscape architecture was essential, especially in the use of correct terminology and plant identification. During the research stage, she sought out former employees who brought in family photographs and added to the oral history collection. She also took on the complex task of organizing the layout planner. Above all, I appreciate her genuine enjoyment of and dedication to this project.

The period photographs reproduced in this book have been preserved in the Reynolda House Archives, and the retrieval of them depended heavily on the skill of the archivists. In this regard, I would like to extend special thanks to Richard Murdock, former archivist, and to Todd Crumley, who has succeeded him as director of archives and library. In our seemingly endless search for the right photograph, Todd never failed us and exercised extraordinary perseverance in scanning the images in the correct format.

I am indebted to Allison Perkins, executive director of Reynolda House Museum of American Art, for encouraging her staff to review and comment on the final manuscript. My gratitude goes to Virginia Holbrook, assistant to the executive director; Sara Smith, director of marketing and communications; and Philip Archer, director of public programs, for their insightful suggestions. Philip added an important piece of information when he identified a previously unknown gentleman in an archival photograph. Knowing that the man is Mario Chamlee, the star tenor of the Metropolitan Opera who performed at Reynolda in 1921, has contributed significantly to the remarkable story surrounding this event.

In addition to readers from the Reynolda staff, I want to thank Michele K. Gillespie, Stroup faculty fellow and Kahle associate professor of history at Wake Forest University, and Camilla Wilcox, curator of education for Reynolda Gardens of Wake Forest University, for their encouraging and helpful suggestions. Articles by Camilla published in the *Gardener's Journal* about Reynolda's gardens and grounds over many years have supplied valuable information that has filtered into this manuscript.

Throughout this manuscript, I have relied heavily on oral histories taken since 1970 of family and people who lived and worked on the estate. For this project, the following descendants of estate employees have contributed their family photographs and reminiscences: Wayne Lash, Brenda Miller, Bynum Fulcher Jr., and the family of Irvin Disher, including his widow, Mozelle, son Irvin Disher Jr., and granddaughter Dana Myer.

I have been fortunate that so many talented and interested people have so generously contributed to this publication.

INTRODUCTION

Reynolda was the creation of Katharine Smith Reynolds (1880–1924), wife of R.J. Reynolds (1850–1918), founder of the R.J. Reynolds Tobacco Company in Winston-Salem, North Carolina. One of the most successful men in the state at the time of their marriage in 1905, R.J. encouraged his young wife to carry out her dream of building a great estate. In 1914, her achievement was acknowledged when the property was officially named Reynolda, suggesting the Latin feminine of Reynolds. Although unusual in its Southern location and feminine ownership, Reynolda was nonetheless part of a national trend. In the early 1900s, the concept of a large house and garden in a rural setting with extensive farming and sporting facilities was central to a nationwide phenomenon called the American Country House Movement.

Katharine envisioned a new ideal of country living—a self-sufficient country estate with a formal garden, model farm, outdoor recreational facilities, and a large-scale bungalow to serve as the family residence. She brought in experts in agriculture, dairying, horticulture, and domestic technologies to manage the estate, and to share advances in these fields with local farmers and visitors from various parts of the country. In easy walking distance of the bungalow, she built a village with modern houses for her estate supervisors, the church minister, school principal, and select members of her own domestic staff.

Katharine's land purchases began in 1906, when she acquired a 106-acre farm, and again after 1909, when she began purchasing a number of farms and tracts of land located 3.5 miles from the center of town. At its peak, the estate amounted to 1,067 acres. The transformation of this patchwork of eroded and worn-out farms into a model, productive country estate proved to be an immense undertaking, but by 1917, the bungalow was ready for occupancy, and the farm had already become widely known as an "experiment station" that provided farmers with demonstrations and reliable information about scientific agriculture.

Between 1910 and 1912, Buckenham and Miller, a New York landscape engineering firm, laid out the grounds, lake, bungalow site, and village. In 1911, Katharine commissioned Philadelphia architect Charles Barton Keen (1868–1931) to begin designing the bungalow. At about the same time, local architect Williard C. Northup (1882–1942) was submitting plans for cottages and overseeing construction of the greenhouses, but after 1913, his work terminated, and Keen received the later commissions. In 1915, Harvard-trained landscape architect Thomas W. Sears (1880–1966) was brought in and provided up-to-date planting designs for the formal gardens, entrances, roadsides, and grounds that consisted of more than 30 buildings and cottages.

Reynolda as Katharine conceived it had but a brief life. R.J. died in 1918, soon after the family moved into its new home. Katharine married again in 1921 but died three years later, leaving her husband, J. Edward Johnston, with a young son. In 1934, the elder Reynolds daughter, Mary Babcock, acquired the property and maintained it until after World War II, when she and her husband, Charles H. Babcock, began to parcel out land for residential development and as donations to educational institutions. The largest of those went to the new campus of Wake

Forest College. Today, Wake Forest University owns the village and gardens under various deed restrictions. The bungalow, now the Reynolda House Museum of American Art, was established under a separate charter as a historical site and museum and affiliated with the university in 2002. Reynolda Historic District, consisting of 178 acres of the original estate, is listed on the National Register of Historic Places.

A large portion of the cultural landscape and historical buildings are still intact, and Reynolda Historic District is open to the public free of charge, allowing thousands of people to benefit from the property each year. When they discover the historical significance of the many familiar sights illustrated and described in this book, they will gain a better understanding of the importance of Reynolda's preservation and restoration.

PHOTOGRAPH LEGEND

Unless otherwise noted, all photographs come from the Reynolda House Museum of American Art Archives. Several photographs were taken by either Barbara Millhouse (BM), Thomas Sears (TS), or Sherold Hollingsworth (SH). Additional photographs were given or loaned to the archives by families and friends of Reynolda:

AD   Albert Drage Jr., son of Albert Drage Sr.
AS   Helen Sigmon Sprinkle, daughter of Adrian Sigmon
BF   Bynum Fulcher Jr., grandson of William Fulcher
EL   Wayne Lash, son of Ed Lash
FP   First Presbyterian Church of Winston-Salem, North Carolina
HM   Brenda Miller, daughter of Harvey Miller
ID   Dana Myer, granddaughter of Irvin Disher

One

MEETING THE

REYNOLDS FAMILY

This c. 1914 photograph shows Katharine and R.J. Reynolds and their four children sitting at a table in their Fifth Street house in Winston-Salem, North Carolina. It was taken at a time when Katharine and R.J. often drove the three miles to Reynolda to oversee the progress of their country estate. The farm had been in operation for two years, the golf course was complete, and their residence, invariably referred to as "the bungalow," was under construction. From left to right, the children are Dick, Mary, Nancy, and Smith.

R.J. Reynolds was 54 years old when he married for the first time. In 1905, the year of his marriage, he was a successful plug tobacco manufacturer—so successful, in fact, that the *Mount Airy News* described him as the wealthiest man in the state. His bride, Katharine Smith, whom he had known since her childhood, grew up in Mount Airy, North Carolina. After attending North Carolina State Normal and Industrial College, which prepared women for the workplace, she had accepted a job as a stenographer at the R.J. Reynolds Tobacco Company. Despite a 30-year age gap, they apparently had a happy marriage. Katharine's sister Ruth Smith explained, "I don't think there was any doubt about the genuine attraction because it was as happy a household as one could imagine. I can't recall ever hearing a cross word or anything disagreeable happening or being said. . . . He was very handsome in that period; he looked like a Spanish don."

Upon returning from their European honeymoon, R.J. and his bride moved into this Queen Anne–style house. Built around 1900, it was located at 666 West Fifth Street, a mile from the tobacco factories. In the evenings after the children went to bed, R.J. and Katharine withdrew to the sitting room in the turret, where they spent many evenings looking over plans for their country estate, Reynolda.

On hot summer days, relatives and friends were drawn to the veranda of the Fifth Street house. This photograph shows, from left to right, R.J. and Katharine Reynolds with nieces Lucy Lybrook Stedman and May Lybrook. At the far right sits brother-in-law James Dunn, who probably strolled over from his house across the street. West Fifth Street was a friendly neighborhood made up of the Reynoldses' relatives and R.J. Reynolds Tobacco Company executives—many of whom were both.

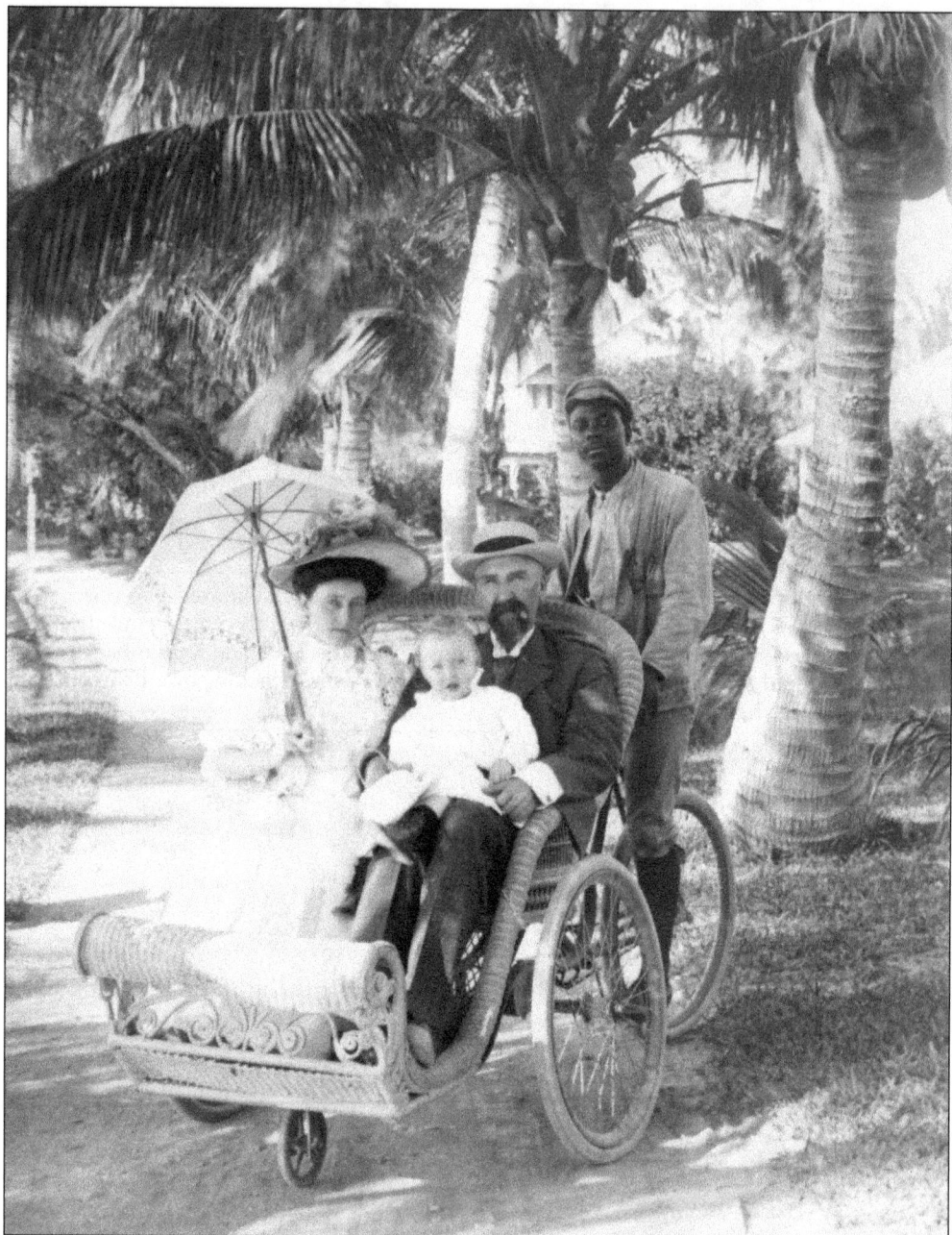

Many of the photographs taken during the early years of the Reynoldses' marriage show the family on trips. In this one, Katharine, R.J., and their two-year-old son, Dick, are in Palm Beach. On March 11, 1908, she wrote to her sister Irene Smith, "This is one of the avenues through which we walk or ride in a rolling chair every day. It is beautiful down here but is getting so warm will have to leave soon." They had already had a pleasant stay at the Hotel Colonial in Nassau and the Royal Palace in Miami. On the way home, they stopped in Jacksonville, where they caught the train north to Greensboro. On March 19, Katharine sent a card to her mother in Mount Airy, saying, "We are now in Greensboro on the train waiting for it to start—reached here about 15 minutes ago. Are all perfectly well now and have had a grand trip."

Wearing a plumed hat and holding her younger son, Smith, Katharine Reynolds looks out from the front seat of her new Buick parked in front of the Fifth Street house. Her grinning son Dick has momentarily usurped the chauffeur's seat. In the rear, R.J., wearing a bowler hat, looks over the heads of daughters Mary and Nancy. They are probably going to visit her parents in Mount Airy, since the rear tires are equipped with chains in case they run into mud and snow. In the summer, the family planned longer trips. Nancy recalled, "I was born in February and in August we drove all the way from Winston to Thousand Islands, Canada, in the car—all the babies and Bum [governess] and Mother and Daddy and the chauffeur. We carried the potty with us, so we didn't have to stop every minute when somebody was full. We went, and then out the window." They did not motor the entire distance, however—they picked up the automobile in Philadelphia and drove north from there.

As a civic leader, R.J. Reynolds was undoubtedly involved in the promotion of the largest aviation show to take place in town before World War I. In 1911, few people had seen an airplane fly, so a program featuring takeoffs, landings, races, and mock battles was thrilling enough to attract large crowds. Wearing a heavy overcoat, R.J. (above) is prepared for a cold, windy day at the airfield. He, like others, was probably disappointed that the near gale-force wind curtailed some of the flying events. In the photograph below, R.J. stands in front of their Royal Tourist and holds Dick's hand on a ferry as they cross what is most likely the Yadkin River. Behind them, also bundled up, are Katharine and Mary. The ferryman and chauffeur stand to the left.

Nancy Reynolds believed that because her father was quite old when he started having children he enjoyed them enormously. Although R.J. died when she was only eight, she "had a warm feeling" when she thought of him. It seems that most people found him kindly and convivial. He knew the names of all his employees, both white and African American, and helped them buy their own homes and encouraged them to buy stock in his company. He had a capacity for hard work and a reputation for fairness in business dealings, which he had undoubtedly learned while working on his father's tobacco farm in Patrick County, Virginia. At age 25, he decided better opportunities were to be had 50 miles south, and with $7,500 in capital, he started his own tobacco manufacturing plant in Winston, North Carolina. He worked tirelessly to build his plug tobacco company, and in 1907 and 1913 he brought out two new products, Prince Albert smoking tobacco and Camel cigarettes, which became leading brands and brought prosperity to an entire region of North Carolina.

Having worked for two years as R.J. Reynolds's private secretary, along with two male secretaries, Katharine Reynolds knew the business well and had no hesitation in pushing for improvements in the workplace. She was said to have influenced the establishment of hot lunches, day care, and literacy classes. Her younger sister Ruth, who frequently stayed in their home, felt that as a wife Katharine continued to play a partnership role, which few wives at that time had attained. "Having been his private secretary, she was well aware of all the mechanics of the company," she explained, "and just continued in an advisory [capacity]. I think she must have felt perfectly free to offer any suggestions she thought of, and he must have felt perfectly free, without taking offense to take it, work it over, and use it or discard it. I think there was real companionship there."

Elizabeth Wade, the switchboard operator at Reynolda, observed that Katharine "loved her children a whole lot. . . . She would sometimes play games with them and entertain them. . . . She was a lovely mother." Lucy Cash, a teacher who lived at the bungalow during the first year of the Reynolda School, said, "She was fond of the children; the girls particularly were very natural with her." This c. 1913 photograph shows Katharine with daughters Nancy (left) and Mary in the Fifth Street house. Nancy explained, "I think Mother was the boss of the house. My father enjoyed us; we were his entertainment, but she handled the discipline."

The chauffeur, who most likely took this photograph, stopped the Royal Tourist on a bridge in a wooded area probably for the family to enjoy a picnic lunch. Katharine is seated on a rock ledge over a stream next to an unidentified boy, and Mary and Nancy, wearing pretty little hats, are seated on the opposite bank. Dick is leaning against the car, and nurse Lizzie Thompson is holding Smith. The location has not been recorded, but it brings to mind one of Nancy Reynolds's recollections about trips to see her grandparents in Mount Airy. "In the early days, it took all day to get to Mount Airy," she explained. "Of course, the cars were slower, and we were really going fast if we went 20 miles an hour. We always took a picnic lunch. . . . We had just forded a stream, and we stopped the car . . . and sat along the side of the road having our picnic lunch."

This photograph of the heavily laden Royal Tourist shows Katharine Reynolds in the front seat on the far right next to the chauffeur. Five other elaborately attired women are seated in the rear. The automobile was decorated for the state convention of the General Federation of Women's Clubs, which was held in Winston in 1912. As head of the hospitality committee, Katharine had offered Sallie Southall Cotton, president of the club, the use of her automobile for the duration of the convention. The Reynoldses' Royal Tourist is adorned with sprigs of pine tied with blue and white ribbon to advertise the presence of these formidable women who were committed to civic and social improvements. The detail at right shows the chauffeur on the left, Katharine on the right, and two unidentified women in the rear.

Katharine's glamour, intelligence, and exceptional business sense were legendary among family, friends, and employees. Her switchboard operator found her "every inch a lady. She was so fine, you would think she was born in a gold pit, the way she deported herself." The teachers who resided in the bungalow during the winter of 1918 noticed characteristics that shed more light on her ability to envision and realize a great estate like Reynolda. Ethel Brock recalled, "She had wonderful ideas, and she was a person who could carry out any project. She was meticulous in her plans for anything she undertook." Another teacher was impressed by her determination and power of concentration—useful characteristics for implementing an ambitious dream.

Two

BUILDING REYNOLDA

The buggy parked at the gardener's cottage belonged to Katharine Reynolds, who has driven from town to inspect one of the first cottages built at Reynolda. Although by 1912, the date of this photograph, Philadelphia architect Charles Barton Keen had been on the job for at least a year, this cottage was designed by local architect Willard C. Northup, who had been working for the Reynoldses on commercial projects downtown.

In 1906, one year after her marriage, Katharine Reynolds purchased her first farm of 106 acres (now the site of the Graylyn Estate) located on the west side of Bethania Road (later Reynolda Road), which runs diagonally through this 1927 aerial view. At first, it was no different from other farms owned by townspeople, but in 1909, a novel use for the land surfaced: R.J. Reynolds wanted to build a golf course on it. A survey showed, however, that a course of only nine holes would take up the entire farm, and he told his wife jokingly that he did not want to put such a good farmer out of business. He advised her to buy more property and suggested that some of the landowners on the east side of the highway might be willing to consider an offer. Over the next 13 years, she made 27 land acquisitions that, by 1914, became known collectively as Reynolda.

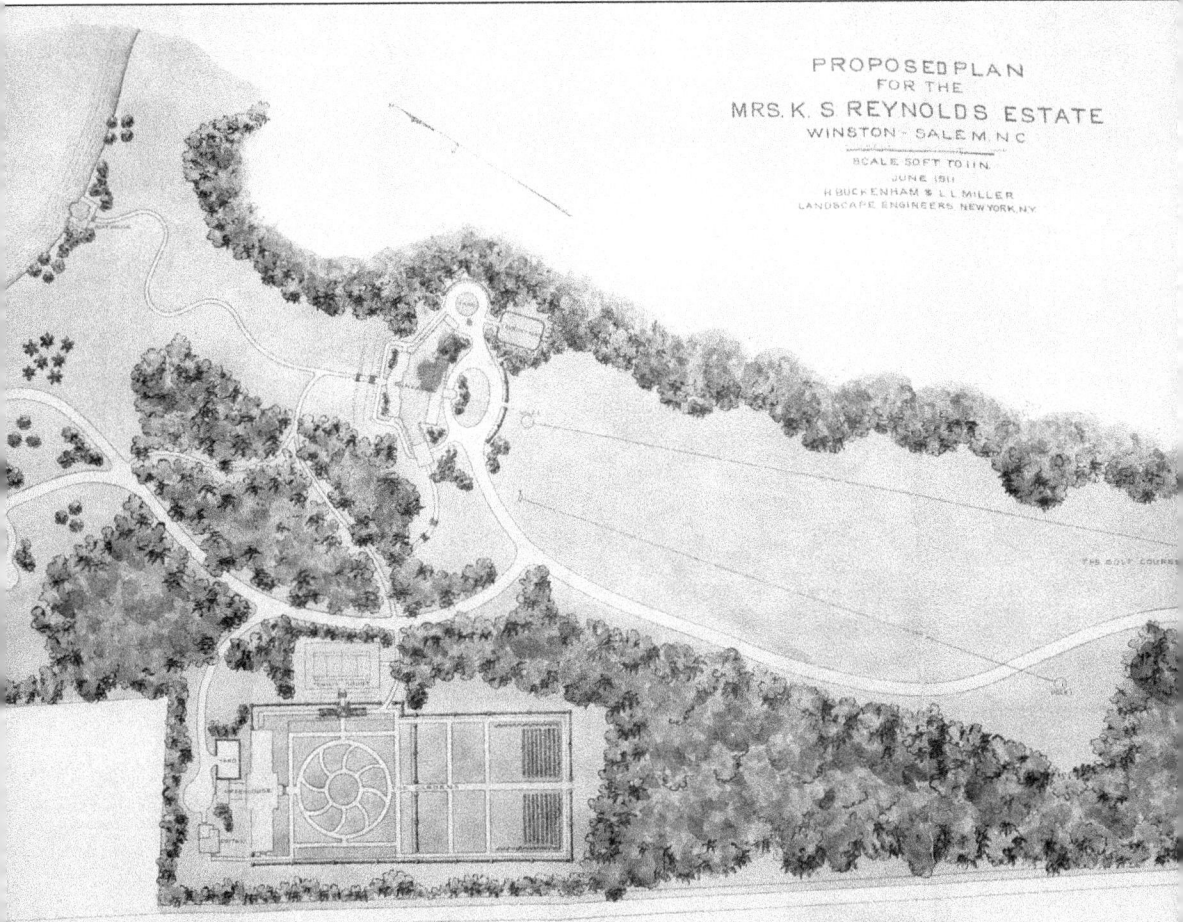

PROPOSED PLAN
FOR THE
MRS. K. S REYNOLDS ESTATE
WINSTON - SALEM, N.C.
SCALE 50 FT TO 1 IN.
JUNE 1911
H. BUCKENHAM & L.L. MILLER
LANDSCAPE ENGINEERS, NEW YORK, N.Y.

In 1910, the New York landscape engineering firm of H.H. Buckenham and L. Miller was commissioned to transform the depleted and eroded land that Katharine was acquiring into a model productive country estate. In June 1911, the firm presented this conceptual plan, only half of which is reproduced here. At this initial stage, the slow pace of land acquisition and the uncertainty of obtaining crucial acreage created impediments in envisioning the estate as a whole. The landscape engineers, for example, had to work around a key tract of unavailable land represented by the empty area at the lower left. Fortunately, on October 5, 1911, five months after this plan was completed, Katharine was able to obtain the critical tract, and new opportunities for her country estate opened up. Already established, however, was the placement of the formal garden and the man-made lake seen in the upper left corner of this map. In the final plan, the first tee of the golf course was moved farther away from the house.

23

In the c. 1910 photograph above, the Reynolds family is enjoying bright winter sunshine on the 79-acre Emory S. Gray farm, the first property to come up for sale on the east side of Bethania Road. Katharine plays in a pile of construction sand with her three children while R.J. gazes north over the unkempt fields towards the site of their future home. Only a few months earlier, R.J. reported that Mr. Knox, a well driller, had tapped into a large water supply in the tree-lined hollow in the background. The same view, shown below, was taken three years later and looks out over the newly completed golf course, which incorporated into its design the natural lay of the land. The soil was so depleted that it took three years of conditioning before seed could be sown for turf.

On August 7, 1912, Katharine wrote to the magazine *American Golfer* requesting the "best book published on the making of golf grounds." The results are evident in this aerial view, in which the first tee is visible south of the cross drive. Since the greens were made of sand, they are easily discernible. The small, kidney-shaped spots are sand traps.

In this informal scene, the Reynolds children and their mother are playing on the golf course near the first tee. The start of the lake road is visible in the background. Low retaining walls made of rock like the one seen above were built to elevate the tees. Civil engineer R.E. Snowden confirmed this in August 1912 when he reported, "We have raised Tee 6 considerably, about 12 inches."

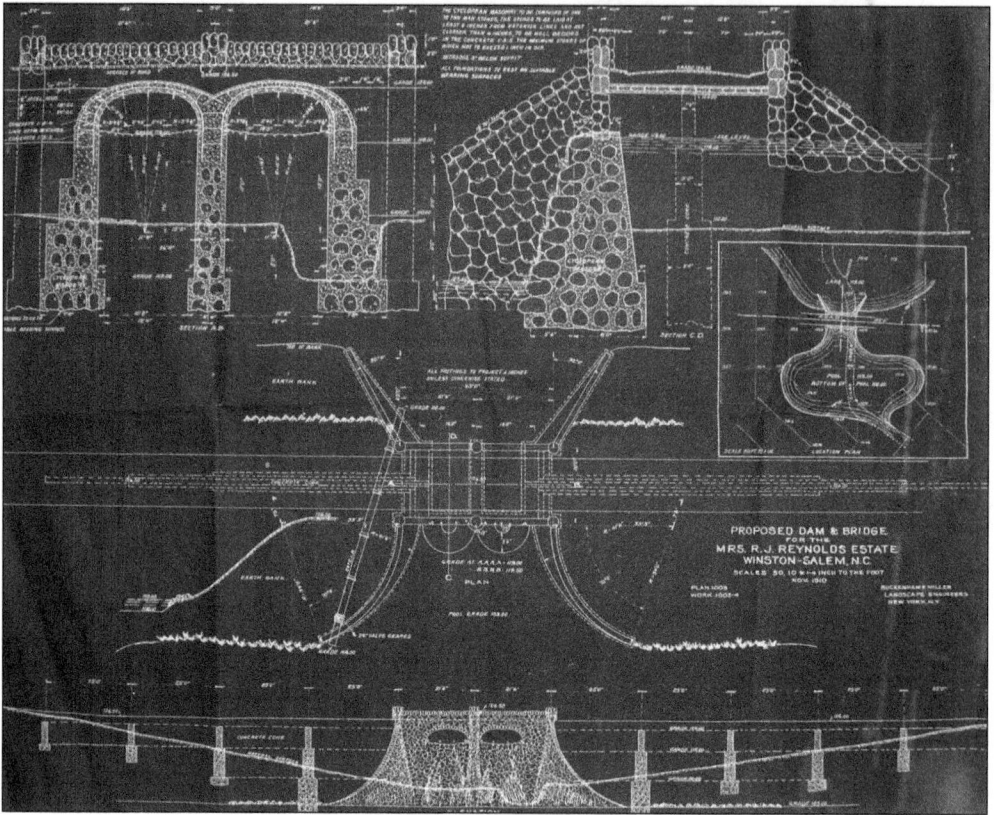

The Buckenham and Miller conceptual plan called for a lake, which entailed building a concrete-core earthen dam at its west end. The blueprint (above) shows the plan and elevations. After the concrete core set, it was faced with rocks excavated from the lake bed. Between the blueprint and the final construction (below) the design of the bridge was changed from a double to a single arch, which required eliminating the central support. The double cascade, however, remained.

The woman at the right is Katharine Reynolds, who has come from town to inspect the progress of the main barn. She was known to have overseen every detail of the construction projects. She specified the required number and size of the horse stalls and even asked architect Charles Barton Keen for the number of bricks needed for the main barn, since they were to be ordered locally.

Facing the camera in a dark suit with a bolero jacket, Katharine Reynolds stands with four members of the oversight committee who have come to inspect the progress of the Reynolda Presbyterian Church. Katharine was said to have spent hours upon hours with the architect and minister to ensure that the design of the interior conformed to the services.

This photograph shows early construction work on the bungalow, which was built of reinforced concrete, a new material that came into use at the turn of the century. It was made by combining the concrete with metal reinforcing rods to give it strength. This c. 1914 photograph shows the wood forms into which the concrete was poured for the footings. After the concrete hardened, the forms were removed.

Taken when the bungalow was under construction, this photograph shows it as a long, low building with two oblique lateral wings. This arrangement was called a "suntrap plan," because it was designed to capture as much sun as possible during winter months. The mules and workmen on the right serve as a reminder that the bungalow, although modern in construction, was nonetheless built entirely by animal and human labor.

The son and namesake of the man in overalls, Bynum Fulcher Sr. (front left), donated this photograph of the contractors to the Reynolda House Archives. Many different trades were used in building the bungalow. According to the architect's assistant, "Everything was done 100 percent correctly by good mechanics. There wasn't a poor mechanic on the job." Contractors came mostly from New York, Philadelphia, Boston, and Lynchburg, Virginia. (BF.)

From 1914 to 1917, when the bungalow was under construction, the Reynolds family drove frequently from town to visit the site of their new home. This photograph shows daughter Nancy in a white hat on the left, Mary in a high-crowned hat standing on a sand pile, and younger son Smith in a middy suit crouched next to a dog at the feet of nurse Lizzie Thompson.

A steam-powered rock crusher (above) was the only piece of heavy construction equipment used in the building of Reynolda. The large flywheel provided the momentum necessary to crush rocks and boulders into gravel of various sizes for concrete, roadbeds, and, in its finest form, for garden paths. Machines like this were quite dangerous, especially for a workforce accustomed to working by hand. It caused at least one recorded injury. William B. Fulcher (left), who had been employed to grade roads, was trying "to put the belt on the motor," when it flipped him. In 1918, after his discharge from the hospital, Katharine Reynolds continued to employ him but in a safer job as night watchman. Seated on the arm of Fulcher's chair, his grandson Bynum accompanied him on his early rounds. As an adult, Bynum gave an oral history sharing his observations of Reynolda during that time. (Left, BF.)

Just as gasoline and electricity are sources of energy today, manpower combined with animal power was the source of energy in the building of Reynolda. "Rocks, rock, rocks were everywhere in evidence," a reporter exclaimed. Teamsters driving mules hitched to buckboards with wooden wheels like this one hauled rocks to construction sites. Admired for their rustic effect, the rocks were used as a substitute for commercial stone.

Good wages and the promise of a better life lured hundreds of men off tenant farms to join the Reynolda workforce. Ellis Pledger walked 20 miles a day to make $9 a week, three times more than wages at home. In 1916, he and his wife, Flora, moved nearby to Five Row, a newly built community for African American farmworkers. Flora thought that it was "the best place" she had ever seen.

A Nissen wagon travels down Reynolda Road (above) past the village entrance, the gardener's cottage, and the farmhouse (used as the men's boarding house until about 1940). In 1916, Katharine Reynolds paid $10,000 to the North Carolina State Highway Department to pave Reynolda Road as far as her estate. According to Reynolda's horticulturist's son Robert Conrad Jr., "Mrs. Reynolds wanted a hard surface road from Summit Street to Silas Creek. State didn't have the money to do it, so she furnished the materials and the state furnished the labor. At that time, all the roads were built by convicts." The photograph below shows the convicts paving Reynolda Road. They are under tight guard. Even so, Katharine's daughter Mary told the story that when she was swimming in the Reynolda lake, she pulled up from the bottom a striped suit discarded by an escaped convict.

During the summer of 1916, when the bungalow was under construction and war was raging in Europe, the Reynolds family pitched camp on the edge of the golf course. It had a roofed dining area, visible in the background of the photograph above, and a kitchen with a concrete platform still in place near the spring-fed brook. Pictured above, from left to right, are daughter Mary, governess Henrietta van den Burg, (better known as "Bum"), daughter Nancy, an unidentified woman, and Katharine Reynolds with one arm akimbo. R.J. holds his son Smith, and in front of them stands older son Dick. The striped tents, below, form the backdrop for children's activities. The Indian headdresses worn by Nancy and Smith were undoubtedly inspired by the legend that the nearby springs were once the site of Native American campgrounds.

In August 1912, Katharine gave these instructions, "The grass [on the golf course] must all be in by September in the best ground, and in the other ground by February 1913. Do not have a weed standing in any of this entire ground." By spring, the golf course was evidently ready for use, and Katharine (left, third from the left) was quick to organize ladies' foursomes. Oral histories record that while the family was still living in town, R.J. often brought his son Dick out to play. The new turf also provided a setting for picnics (below). This one appears to be a family gathering, with R.J. standing prominently with his arms crossed and Katharine ascending the hill on the right.

Three

BUNGALOW GROUNDS

On the north facade of the bungalow, an open porch sweeps out over a semicircular, boxwood-bordered terrace that overlooks the 16-acre lake. Its encircling trellis supports wisteria vines, which dropped lavender, pendant-shaped blossoms over the porch in spring. In the foreground, roses tumble playfully over the retaining wall. (TS.)

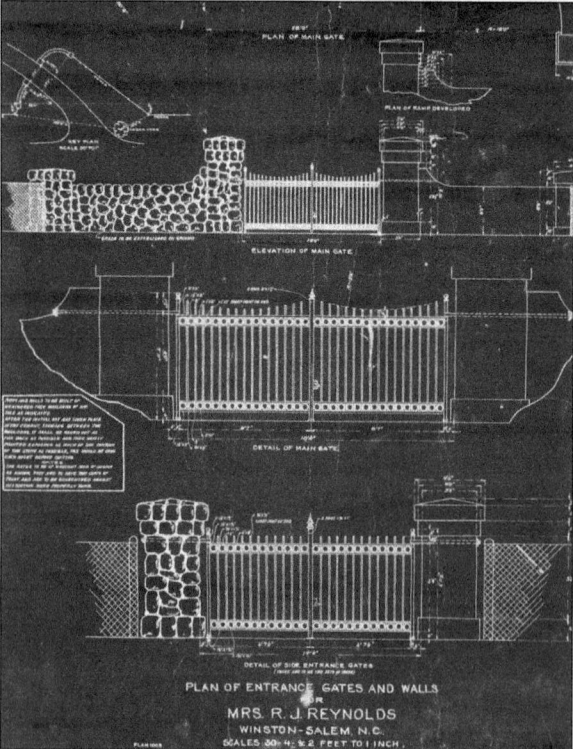

PLAN OF ENTRANCE GATES AND WALLS
FOR
MRS. R. J. REYNOLDS
WINSTON-SALEM, N.C.

The 1911 blueprint at left shows the Buckenham and Miller drawings for the entrance gate that is seen above with an automobile passing through. Its bleak appearance can be explained by the delay in landscaping. In January 1913, Katharine Reynolds wrote impatiently to one of the partners, Louis Miller, "Your plan shows no planting on the outside of the gate, but I felt sure that you intended to put some in there. . . . We have a pile of rock there at present." This is the first sign of her impatience with Miller. By April 1915, he had been replaced by Thomas W. Sears, a Harvard-trained landscape architect recommended by Keen. Sears designed the formal gardens and the planting around the bungalow, cottages, and buildings in the village. He continued to work for Katharine until her death, and subsequently for her daughter, Mary Babcock.

Chauffeur Cleve Williams, nurse Lizzie Thompson, and the Reynolds children (above) try to keep a sheep—probably Bob, the pet lamb—from following them through the front gate. After Bob grew too large for his pen, he was sent to the sheepfold at Katharine's first farm (below) on the west side of Reynolda Road, where Graylyn Estate is located today. Bob, however, did not forget his family. When the children visited the farm, he would break from the flock and run to greet them. Sheep were rarely raised in the South because they were vulnerable to packs of wild dogs, but under the watchful eye of shepherd M.S. Yow and his dog, Seabreeze, the Reynolda flock grew in size from 25 to 216 in four years.

Upon entering Reynolda, the bungalow appears at a distance of nearly a half-mile (above). After running along open ground at the edge of the golf course, the drive enters a shady grove of trees, which conceals the bungalow from view. The contrasts between light and dark, opened and closed, are carefully orchestrated along the drive to provide a succession of pleasing sensations. In addition, early spring brings a ravishing display of daffodils covering the woodland floor. Emerging from the grove of trees (below), the bungalow bursts into view again through loosely planted cedars. The road swings left toward the bungalow entrance and another road takes a sharp right toward the two-and-a-half-mile lake drive.

The original driveway (above) entered the forecourt of the bungalow from the west. Although pine groves covered the hillside at the rear, the front was completely barren. Consequently, shade trees were planted extensively. The tall tree left of the center is probably the one that was photographed below being hauled from the woods on a mule-drawn wagon. Years later, Robert Conrad Jr., the horticulturist's son, recalled, "The men would dig up a 50-year-old tree with a huge root ball. They hauled it on the back of this number 14 truck. It didn't have a battery; it didn't have a starter. It ran on a magneto, and I saw one man break his arm trying to crank it. But they put the tree in the ground and it lived." (Above, TS.)

The original driveway looped around a grass island and under the porte-cochère, which sheltered the front entrance. The bungalow's colonnaded porch was built nearly on grade to minimize the transition between outdoors and indoors. At the far side of the turnaround, the hedge opened to a flagstone walk leading to a side door. (TS.)

Automobile passengers disembarked beneath this porte-cochère and entered the bungalow through either screen or glass doors depending on the season. In the spring and fall, they were likely to find the porch entirely open. Visible in this photograph are American pillar roses, which were trained to climb trellises and run along the eaves, where breezes could catch their scent and waft it through the house. (TS.)

In May 1918, when Katharine Reynolds was in Philadelphia and missing the glorious spring at Reynolda, a friend tried to console her by writing, "We are enjoying Reynolda for you. . . . The dogwoods, cedars, and pines have never been more beautiful, and the azaleas around the bungalow have been lovely." She must have been referring to the planting along the driveway (above), which is shown curving gracefully away from the forecourt. Since the driveway was shifted to the east wing in 1936, this view no longer exists, but the Thomas Sears planting plan (below) preserves the layout at this location. Waving beds of azaleas border the drive, and cedars are grouped to fill the corner where the west wing meets the central block. The plan also specifies a number of oak trees on the lawn.

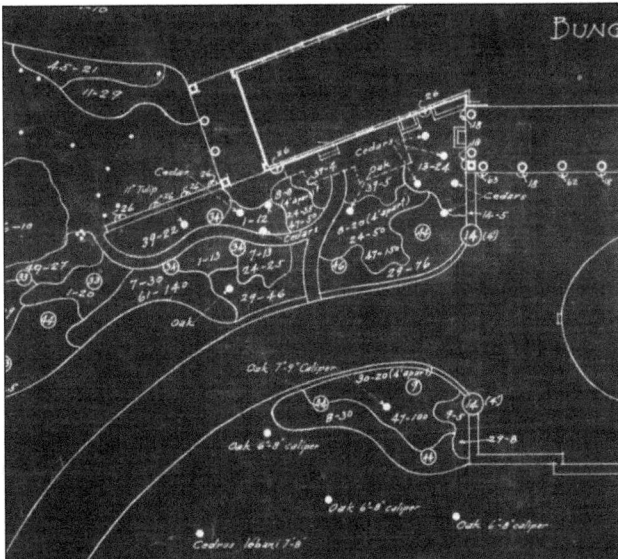

The forecourt was often the preferred spot to snap photographs before visitors departed. In the group above, only Katharine Reynolds (standing on the left) and daughter Nancy (in the middle) can be identified. The family's Pierce Arrow is parked under the porte-cochère. Handwritten notations on the snapshot below, dated 1919, indicate that a tire on the Pierce Arrow has been punctured just outside Durham on the way to Atlantic City. Robert Holden, the chauffeur, and young Dick Reynolds (in knickers) change the tire, while Smith and Nancy (wearing middy outfits) and an unidentified woman wait by the roadside. Since motoring was still a relatively new mode of transportation, roads were riddled with ruts and gullies, making flats and breakdowns frequent. Consequently, chauffeurs were expected to be good mechanics.

The service drive (right) veers off towards the kitchen entrance (below). The roads have not yet been paved. In November 1917, farm superintendent Clint Wharton reported, "We finished putting rock on the new road at the Bungalo [sic] this p.m., have some rolling to do on it yet and then it is ready for the surfacing to go on." It is unclear which road he was referring to, but it was probably the unpaved roads near the bungalow. According to Al Drage Jr., the greenhouse supervisor's son, the Reynolda workforce paved all the roads. "They were graded first with drag pans and mules. They had a huge tar vat. Rock came out of the quarry. A steamroller leveled and compacted the mixture. These were called macadamized roads."

Since one of the allures of living in a bungalow was its openness to the outdoors, Charles Barton Keen designed the new Reynolds home with ample porches and numerous entryways. The flagstone walk (left) leads to the screen door at the east end of the entrance porch and also to the inconspicuous side entrance, which in 1936 was converted to the front door. On the second story, shutters and awnings shut out the sun while still allowing air to enter. The walk veering to the left continues in the photograph below, where it leads to an opening in the boxwood hedge bordering the forecourt.

Springtime drew the family to the porch at the east end of the bungalow (above) to take in the succession of flowering shrubs and trees—first with drifts of daffodils brightening the woodland floor (below), then the glorious white and pink azaleas and dogwoods, each in their timely fashion, and finally mountain laurel. Overall, this created a sequence of changing color throughout the spring. In early summer, when leaves were easing into green, the large, bowl-shaped blooms of the *magnolia grandiflora* opened up. The porch itself was enlisted in the parade of spring blossoms; flowering vines were trained up trellises and across the eaves to frame the view of the naturalized woodland. (Both, TS.)

Thomas Sears designed the pool garden (left) as the focal point of the north side of the east wing. The round water lily pool is aligned with the library porch, which is guarded by a pair of tall cedars in the Italianate mode. On the stepping stone path leading to the pool garden, Dick and Smith Reynolds (below) stand near a bollard light, many of which were installed on the grounds to illuminate paths at night. At the time of their installation, Katharine did not want R.J. to know how much they cost. "Just go ahead and put them in," she told Robert Gibson, the electrician. Lighting gardens and woodlands might have been an extravagance, but it encouraged strolling in the night air, a dramatic change from earlier times when people feared its effects. (Left, TS.)

The north facade of the bungalow was dramatically sited to overlook a steep incline, which descended to a 16-acre lake. The semicircular porch swells outward to a grass terrace with curved steps breaking through a retaining wall and spilling out over the lawn. Designed to soften the transition between house and grounds, this architectural feature reflects the influence of prominent English architect Edwin L. Lutyens (1869–1944). (TS.)

In May 1918, niece Senah Critz wrote to Katharine Reynolds, "We went to your house Monday evening. The porches were lighted and the children were out there studying." The children made such good use of the lake porch that it was sometimes called the children's play porch. The ages of Nancy and Mary in this photograph suggest that it was taken soon after the family moved in.

From the lake porch, which was a favorite gathering place on summer afternoons, the family looked out over this view enlivened in the middle distance by a body of water. The tall cedar was one of a pair framing the vista and marking the point at which the woods give way to open ground. The hill slopes steeply down to the lake and on the far side it rises again to woods screening distant orchards, vineyards, and fields of wheat, corn, and oats.

North of the pool garden on the edge of the woods, a grove of long-leafed pines shades a rustic pavilion overlooking the tennis court. A wire fence covered with climbing roses encloses the court. It was one of two courts on the estate; the other was located across Reynolda Road near the athletic field, which is the present site of Summit School.

48

Four

LAKE AND BOATHOUSE

Looking across the tranquil surface of the 16-acre lake, this view shows the boathouse nestled into the shore and shaded by a grove of trees. Silhouetted against the woodland, the hillside behind rises up to the semicircular lake porch on the north facade of the bungalow.

This 1916 panorama shows a serene body of water, which appears to fit so comfortably into the contours of the land that it might have been there for centuries. When it was taken, however, the lake was four years old. Beginning in August 1911, a large work force cleared the land of trees and stumps, dug the lake bed, and built a dam across the creek to contain the water as it rose. Following the shoreline,

the road curls gracefully into the turnaround to the boathouse and then veers up the hill towards the west wing of the bungalow. Buckenham and Miller laid out the circulation system in serpentine roads, which provide access to various parts of the estate. The boathouse is visible on the left, and the barns are situated on the right.

This photograph of the lake was published in the October 1917 issue of *House Beautiful*. The caption read, "Sixty thousand daffodil bulbs were naturalized around this lake, and in blooming time the place is thronged with visitors." In the distance, the bungalow is visible from its commanding site on the hill above the boathouse. Over time, the lake became silted-in, and today it functions as a protected wetland.

This view looks across the lake toward the dam, which was designed as an arched bridge to give the impression that the lake continues on the other side, but in fact it disguises a spillway forming a double cascade. Running over the spillway, a dirt road was the start (or finish) of the road around the lake. Today it is a paved footpath connecting Reynolda Village to the campus of Wake Forest University. (TS.)

One of the more picturesque features of the grounds is visible from the field below the dam, where a double waterfall flanked by cascading roses forms the backdrop to a pool. It was given a concrete bottom and a dock to make it appealing to village residents, who described it as the community swimming pool. (TS.)

Marie Drage, wife of the greenhouse supervisor, stands on the dock of the concrete bottom pool below the dam—a favorite swimming area for estate employees. Al Drage Jr., Marie's son, learned to swim here when he was three years old. He recalled, "They had a boardwalk down there and steps to go down to the water. They cleaned it out once a year." (AD.)

On May 25, 1921, *Hiawatha: The Indian Passion Play*, based on Henry Wadsworth Longfellow's poem, was staged on the sandy bank of the lake at the left of the apple orchard (above). It was produced by the Reynolda School and performed by students and village residents (below). Leading parts went to Mary Reynolds, who played Minnehaha, and Bowman Gray Jr., who played Hiawatha. Many photographs have survived—all taken in the daytime—but the play was held in the evening to an audience of 5,000 seated on the opposite shore. As darkness fell, Robert Gibson, the Reynolda electrician, had an opportunity to display his skills at theatrical lighting. The local newspaper praised it as "one of the most beautiful outdoor events in the history of Winston-Salem."

Dance interludes were performed between the acts of *Hiawatha*. Nancy Reynolds can be spotted among the wind phantoms (above) dancing in filmy homemade gowns and daisy chain crowns pulled low over their brows. Taking their cue from modern dancer Isadora Duncan, they frolicked and swayed barefoot on the grass. Participants complained that only pretty girls were selected as wind phantoms. The unfortunate fireflies (below) had to wear brown burlap sacks and run around in the shrubbery switching flashlights on and off.

Charles Barton Keen's plans for the boathouse have not survived, but it must have been built before January 1913, the year when Katharine Reynolds reported the lake was lacking one-and-a-half feet of water. Its half-timbered gables and arched plank shutters fall in line with the popular Arts and Crafts style. Adding to its charm, the roof is crowned with a cupola and spire.

Matt Smith, Katharine Reynolds's brother, and four unidentified women pose for the camera in front of the boathouse. The diamond-paned boathouse window on the right reflects the medieval aspects of the Arts and Crafts style. The sunken brick terrace has not yet been built, which would date this photograph before 1916, a time when Katharine was using this area for church picnics.

56

At the far end of the lake (above), the woods grew up to the water's edge, giving this area a wild and secluded character. Al Drage Jr. recalled taking a boat out at night with his father "to frog gig around the edges of the lake." Al Drage Sr. (right) paddles a canoe on the lake, which was stocked with smallmouth bass and perch to encourage fishing. The Reynolda School teachers, who were living in the manse at the time, looked to the lake to supply their dinner. According to Ethel Brock, by the end of the week when their money ran out, "they would go fishing down at the lake and have fresh fish for Friday night supper." (Right, AD.)

This drawing of the proposed boathouse terrace (above) was sent to R.J. and Katharine Reynolds in February 1916. They had selected the boathouse, built a number of years earlier, as the location for the R.J. Reynolds Tobacco Company's Fourth of July celebration. In order to accommodate the large number of guests, Thomas Sears had been asked to design a terrace, which he envisioned as a sunken garden. The drawing was closely followed in the final construction (below). Its main feature was a wall fountain with a lion's head spout feeding water into a semicircular trough. Its use was not limited to the daytime. With a flip of a switch, small electric wall lanterns gave off enough light for nighttime gatherings.

From the lake porch, a long grass slope led to wide steps descending to the boathouse terrace. Pale blue, bearded iris grew out of beds in the brick pavement laid in a basket-weave pattern. A detail from a 1916 panorama (below) shows the salesmen for the R.J. Reynolds Tobacco Company and their wives arriving at the lake for the annual Fourth of July barbecue. The guests walk towards the boathouse, where a luncheon was served featuring barbecue from homegrown Tamworth hogs accompanied by vegetables and fruit produced at Reynolda. The salesmen came by train from states east of the Mississippi River.

A stepping stone path led from the boathouse a short distance along the lakeshore to a cove where a flat-bottom boat was moored (above). Numerous reports indicate that employees used it for fishing. Shober Hendrix, the second electrician, recalled, "I'd go out there in the evenings after I got off work, and fish. . . . It was a good way to relax. At that time, the lake out here was beautiful." This view looks off to the southeast end, which ran nearly up to the edge of the outdoor swimming pool. Occasionally, the lake yielded surprises. Ed Lash, who grew up in Five Row, reported, "My second son caught one of the biggest fish that was ever caught in the lake—a carp three feet long." (Left, EL.)

An outdoor swimming pool, built originally as an irrigation basin, was spring-fed and located in a wooded area at the south end of the lake, visible in the detail at right. Since it was only a short distance downstream from the campsite, it was used during the summer of 1916 for swimming. In 1918, after moving into the bungalow, Katharine Reynolds wanted the pool to have a more festive setting and asked Thomas Sears to draw up plans for improvements. He added stone steps to give access to the pump house roof and an exedra—the semicircular seat built in the stone wall (above). A striped awning provided shade for onlookers, and a slide provided excitement for children. Japanese lanterns were added for nighttime use.

The photographer caught Mary Reynolds just before she slid into the water. Although her long legs make her look older, she is probably not yet 14, since her mother required all girls over 14 to wear black stockings with their bloomer swimsuits. Bathing suit styles were in transition, so the requirement seemed old-fashioned to some girls, but if they did not bring their stockings, they were not allowed to swim.

In May 1918, when Thomas Sears was designing a more habitable setting for the swimming pool, he sent Katharine Reynolds blueprints of this bridge. The foreman described it as a "stone arch over stream leading toward lake." A wet, wooded area like this was likely to be inhabited by all sorts of creatures, so this skirmish caught by the camera was probably a frequent event. The inscription on the snapshot reads, "killing a snake."

Five

GREENHOUSES AND FORMAL GARDENS

This view looks across the formal garden from the entrance pergola towards the palm house. Its thick white columns relate it architecturally to the bungalow. Reminiscent of the garden architecture of Southern Italy, it conjures up images of classically attired women in a vine-covered shelter gazing across the Mediterranean, a subject popular with artists of the period and one that justified the garden being referred to as an Italian or Classical Revival garden. (TS.)

The public entered the gardens through the palm house (above). It was completed in 1913, a number of years before the formal gardens, which were still under construction when these ladies (left) came for what appears to be a public event. The occasion was probably the opening of the greenhouses, although it might also have been the first chrysanthemum show held annually for the benefit of the Red Cross. The little girl peering at the photographer (left) is daughter Mary at about five years old in front of the palm house. The formal gardens were not planted in their final form for another five years. (Above, TS.)

Irvin Disher was a tall, handsome young man in 1911, when he came to work at Reynolda. One of his earliest memories was the arrival from Philadelphia of 44 rare Japanese cherry trees sent from Andorra Nurseries. After the departure of the Drages, he became supervisor of the greenhouses, where many of the plants for the formal gardens were propagated. In the days before refrigerated railroad cars transported produce from Florida, a large portion of the greenhouses was given over to raising vegetables and fruit. At Reynolda, cantaloupes ripened at Christmas and mushrooms were grown in beds of loam in the dark cellar. Disher lived on the outskirts of the property, where he could grow his own food and raise hogs. His house (below) still stands on land donated in 1951 to Wake Forest for its new campus. (Above, ID; below, SH.)

The palm house looks out to the avenue of cryptomeria (above) forming the central axis of the garden. It terminates at the fountain pergola (below), which screens the Greenhouse Garden from the Fruit, Cut Flower, and Nicer Vegetable Garden. Sometimes called Japanese cedars, cryptomeria trees can grow very tall, but they do not have the longevity in a southern climate that they would have in their native Japan. Consequently the original trees declined, and those in the garden today resembling the young cryptomeria in this early photograph have been cultivated from cuttings taken from the originals. The brick and stucco water lily fountain (below) is surrounded on three sides by a retaining wall that supports an elevated level upon which three pergola-connected teahouses offer shelter and a view of the garden. (Both, TS.)

Both of these views look across a grass panel lying at cross axis to the avenue of cryptomeria. The photograph above shows the variation in levels, which divides the garden into distinct sections without obscuring vistas from one part to another. Arrival at the sunken garden is announced by the trickle of water from a lion's head fountain nestled between a pair of brick steps, which were illuminated in the evening by bollard lights, one of which is visible on the far right. Taking advantage of the stage-like effect, Reynolda School children performed a number of operettas and plays at this location, one of which was Shakespeare's A Midsummer Night's Dream. The entrance pergola is echoed by a smaller pergola (below) terminating the cross axis at the western end. (Both, TS.)

Steps from the entrance pergola descend to a grass panel (above) running parallel to the avenue of cryptomeria. Long beds of irises and peonies, which advance the Asian theme already established by the cryptomeria and Japanese cherry trees, break up the grass panel. This same view (below) was taken after the weeping cherry trees had matured and shaded the flower beds. By selecting ornamental cherries as the spring feature of her garden, Katharine Reynolds had overruled landscape architect Thomas Sears, whose planting plans had specified crepe myrtles. Family members believe that the mayor of Tokyo's donation of 3,020 cherry trees to Washington, DC, in 1912 influenced her substitution. Most of those were white-blossomed Yoshino cherries, but the gift also included the pink weeping variety, called Higan, which Katharine selected for Reynolda. (Above, TS.)

Rather than planning the formal gardens as an extension of the main residence, which landscape architects widely advocated, Katharine Reynolds sited her gardens as an extension of the greenhouses, where they could be seen from Reynolda Road and accessed by the public without disturbing the privacy of the family. Despite this departure from the norm, their clear spatial divisions and axial arrangements reflect the latest fashion in garden design. Described as Classical Revival or Italian, the formal gardens were planned along a central axis that ties the ornamental garden to the vegetable garden. A cross axis divides the formal garden into four enclosures called parterres or, as renowned English gardener Gertrude Jekyll called them, garden rooms

An opening in the perennial border leads into the blue and yellow parterre, which is one of four garden rooms flanking the central cryptomeria avenue. In the blue and yellow garden, wisteria standards introduced the color theme of blue, which was repeated in the beds of asters, grape hyacinths, larkspurs, phloxes, plumbagos, and veronicas. The yellow was furnished by calendulas, coreopsis, gaillardias, heleniums, helianthus, rudbeckias, and daylilies. With the addition of annuals as fillers, these bulbs and perennials provided continuous blooms throughout the summer. (TS.)

This view looks south through the rose garden to the teahouses, which divide the ornamental garden from the vegetable garden. Nearly 300 varieties were planted in the two parterres devoted to roses. At the center of each bed, a rose standard was trained in an upright form. Planted around it were hybrid teas, hybrid perpetuals, and multiflora roses. (TS.)

Across the central avenue of cryptomeria, the pink and white parterre was planted with four standard deutzias. The soft pink of their blossom-laden branches established the delicate tone of the floral plantings. Beds of pink perennials such as yarrow, windflower, aster, astilbe, bleeding heart, and hollyhocks were mixed with white ones such as columbine, glory-of-the-snow, candytuft, iris, Madonna lily, narcissus, and phlox, which assured blooms from May to October. In midsummer, hollyhocks (below) became the main feature of the pink and white parterre. The young weeping cherry trees, which would have bloomed several months earlier, rise above the other plantings in the background. Although the layout of the beds is formal, flowers spill out luxuriantly over the grass paths, concealing their strict geometry. (Both, TS.)

The spring display of tulips has drawn the Reynolds children to the formal gardens in this early photograph that was probably taken around 1916. The tulips were filling in while the final planting plans were being worked out. Behind them, a stucco retaining wall with brick coping supports the higher level of the teahouses and vegetable gardens.

This photograph shows Bynum Fulcher Sr., a former Reynolda construction worker and later a mechanics foreman for the R.J. Reynolds Tobacco Company, with three unidentified women in front of a teahouse overlooking the fountain. They probably walked over to the gardens after church. The above-ankle length of the skirts dates this photograph around 1918, which was the time when Bynum's father, William Fulcher, who had been injured in an accident, was hired as night watchman. (BF.)

72

In the early years, the teahouses (above left) were enveloped in a dense array of climbing hydrangea, sweet autumn clematis, and turquoise vine, which is related to the grape and has berries ripening in a sequence from turquoise to purple. Originally lit by lanterns (above right) and furnished with black wooden tables in a Japanese-inspired style (on exhibit at the Reynolda House Museum of American Art), the five shelters provided shaded areas for afternoon tea. The vine-covered pergola (right) connecting the three teahouses surrounding the water lily fountain provided a modicum of shade on hot summer days. It also served as a screen between the ornamental garden and the vegetable garden. (Above left and below right, TS; above right, BM.)

Thomas Sears's planting plans dated February 1921 indicate that the Fruit, Cut Flower, and Nicer Vegetable Garden (above) was planted four years after the family moved into the bungalow. More than 150 varieties of plants including espaliered and dwarf fruit trees were cultivated in this garden during Katharine Reynolds's lifetime. Twenty varieties of bunch grapes, several of which are still producing, were trained against the post-and-rail fences. Edible plants such as strawberries, currants, figs, and rhubarb were also grown, but these represent only a small portion of the total food production at Reynolda. Since arrangements of fresh flowers were considered essential to a respectable home, a cutting garden (below) ran along the central path between a turf border and wooden fence. It supplied gladioli, snapdragons, ageratums, and other annuals. (Both, TS.)

Built in 1921 for daughters Mary and Nancy Reynolds, the playhouse (above) overlooks the vegetable garden. With its simulated thatched roof, settles, and flower-filled window boxes, it resembles a rural English cottage. In this period, providing young girls with a playhouse was not regarded as frivolous. According to the periodical *Country Life in America*, it gave them a "sense of ownership and responsibility," which was believed to "develop character." Steps from the playhouse descend to a rose-covered arch (right) marking one of a number of entrances to the vegetable garden. The iron arches once supported 14 varieties of tea roses, some of which have survived and produce a profusion of pink tea-scented clusters that bloom in late spring and early summer. (Above, TS.)

The view above looks north past the teahouses to the greenhouses and Reynolda village beyond. The smokestack rises from the heating plant at the north end of the village. Made of finely crushed gravel from the granite quarry, the path forms the central axis of the gardens connecting the formal garden to the vegetable garden. At the opposite end, it appears to terminate at a shelter but in fact extends as a grass panel (left) beyond the garden boundary into the woods. It reaches as far as the log cabin, which the Reynolds boys claimed as their clubhouse. It was bordered on both sides with cedars, and on the Thomas Sears blueprints, it was given the name Cedar Walk. (Above, TS.)

Six

Village East of Reynolda Road

This detail of a 1916 panorama shows the entrance to the village on the east side of Reynolda Road. The two-story white house on the left is the gardener's cottage, the center building is the office (later post office), and the greenhouses are on the right. These buildings and virtually all new buildings on the estate share the same cheerful color scheme of light green roofs and white stucco walls.

In the above 1927 aerial view of the greenhouse court, the office building (later post office) is visible in its original location on an island in the center. A pair of cedars gives prominence to its front entrance, and foundation plantings soften its perimeter. Opposite it on the north, a long building completed in 1919 was used for the school and later for offices. On the south, two large greenhouses and one smaller one stretch out from both sides of the central palm house. The photograph of the school building (below) shows the London plane trees, relatives of the American sycamore, around the greenhouse court. Sixteen were planted, but one turned out to be a sycamore. All but one of the originals, which were planted around 1913, have survived.

The office, designed in 1912 by local architect W.C. Northup, had two entrances: a portico entrance facing Reynolda Road (above) and a side entrance (below). According to the July 7, 1917, issue of the local newspaper, the building not only contained farm superintendent Clint Wharton's office but also a common reading room with a beamed ceiling and a brick fireplace "for the men of the village." It was soon converted to office space, however, since after 1918, both Robert Conrad, the horticulturist, and Jim Mahoney, the plumber, were working out of this building. Sometime after 1919, the front rooms became a federal post office, where postmistress Mattie Frye sorted letters with no street numbers or zip codes—the address was merely "Reynolda, NC."

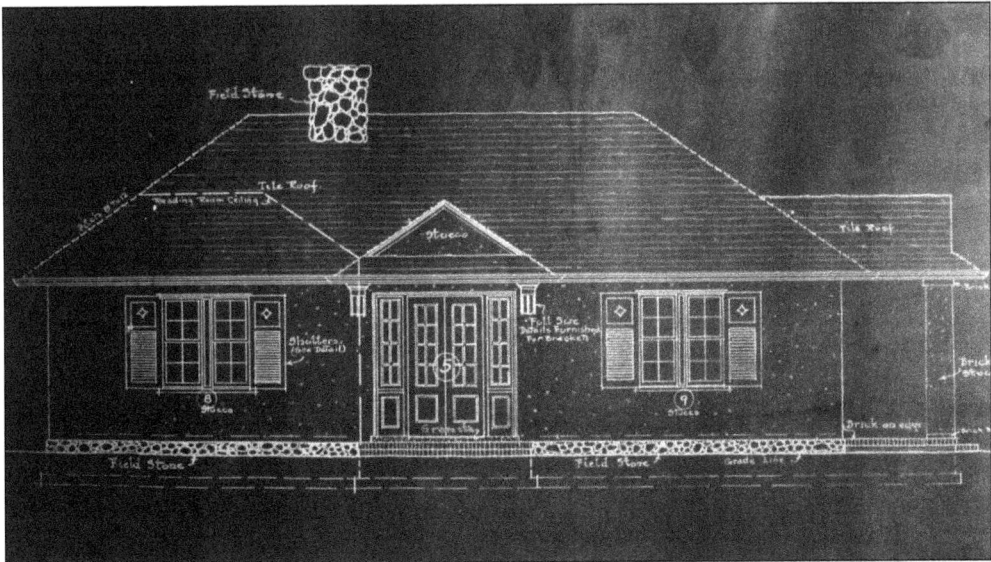

The first greenhouse supervisor was Frederick Martin, who lived across from the greenhouses in the gardener's cottage (above). He and his wife pose outside their cottage near the pergola shading the front door (below). Their life together at Reynolda was idyllic until Frederick, who was English, left to enlist in the armed forces during World War I. On August 21, 1917, Katharine Reynolds received a letter from his wife with the news that he had been killed in action. "His major writes me that his death was instantaneous," she explained, "and that he died a hero's death. That is as it may be, but I know that I have been called upon to give up a life that was very dear and precious to me."

Farm superintendent Clint Wharton and his dog Frank (above) pause in front of the garage, where the family automobiles were stored. In the aerial view below, the garage is at a right angle to the long schoolhouse at the lower center. The line of houses facing Reynolda Road on the far left, from bottom to top, are the gardener's cottage, horticulturist's cottage, farmhouse, and dairyman's cottage. Nearly concealed by a grove of cedars, the servants' cottage is located on the corner at the lower right, and the mule barn is the long shed forming part of the boundary of the paddock. The group of barns including the dairy, stables, and silos stretches across the hill at the right. On the west side of the secondary road are the garage, cattle barn, corn shed, and smokehouse. The chauffeur's cottage stands on the far corner near the heating plant.

The bungalow had been completed for more than a year when Charles Barton Keen began designing a new office building (above) opposite the greenhouses. It was not destined immediately, however, for administrative use. The school that Katharine Reynolds started in 1918 had expanded, and to accommodate the increased enrollment, she turned her new office space into classrooms and hired J. Edward Johnston (above right) as principal. Reflecting her belief in progressive education, Johnston designed a curriculum including foreign languages, drama, music, and art, along with traditional subjects. Nothing of this sort was offered in public schools. One student recalled, "We had a mixture of village folk, Winston-Salem kids, and children from rural areas." Tuition for rural students was paid by the county, making it a semi-public school. Children in Nancy Reynolds's class (below) pose in front of the school building.

C.M. "Mack" Campbell, the second principal of Reynolda School, stands between, from left to right, Ethel Brock (later Mrs. A.T. Sloan), Frances Morris, and Minnie Lou Kelly, teachers living in the manse next to the church. Ethel Brock was hired by former principal J. Edward Johnston, who telephoned her in the summer of 1919 and told her he "had to find up to eight teachers in a hurry." He must have been successful, since the school opened in the fall. Johnston, who later became Katharine Reynolds's second husband, stayed only one year. Campbell, who occupied the gardener's cottage next to the school, succeeded him and stayed until the school closed in 1923. George (Buck) Wharton, chauffeur and mechanic, (below) looks out the window of the bus marked "The Reynolda School." It is parked in front of the heating plant.

Robert Conrad (left) began work at Reynolda in 1913, at age 17. After serving in the Marines during World War I, he earned a degree in horticulture from the University of Maryland and returned to Reynolda to oversee the landscaping for the next 50 years. In 1923, he married Sadie Trotter, who taught second grade at the Reynolda School. They lived in this cottage (above), overlooking Reynolda Road. All cottages were landscaped with shade trees and flowering shrubbery, but the Conrad cottage is the only one photographed after the planting had matured. In later years, when Sadie urged him to buy their own place, Robert rejected the idea. "Sadie," he said, "I can't leave Reynolda." He had arrived at Reynolda as a young man and had been there all his life.

The dairyman's cottage (above) overlooks Reynolda Road. Its first occupant was unrecorded, but in 1920, Adrian Sigmon was hired as dairy foreman and moved into it with his bride, Nelle Holleman (right), who had been teaching at the Reynolda School. Adrian had gained firsthand experience on his family's farm in Hickory, North Carolina, and attended North Carolina A&M College (now North Carolina State University). According to his daughter, he "did not milk the cows. He was up where the product was—the milk. He fixed the milk and the butter and all that and got it ready to be delivered." They raised seven children in this five-room cottage. Although cramped, they considered it comfortable because it was equipped with modern conveniences like electricity, indoor plumbing, hot and cold running water, steam heat, and a telephone. These were rarities in rural areas at the time. (Right, AS.)

John Craig Carter, born in Yadkinville, North Carolina, managed the bungalow for two generations of the Reynolds family. He began work as part-time valet for R.J. Reynolds at the Fifth Street house and was eventually promoted to majordomo. His wife, Marjorie Goins Carter, a graduate of a two-year college, worked as an upstairs maid. In 1917, after the family moved to Reynolda, the Carters (left) lived in the servants' cottage (below), located on the corner where the road turns up the hill to the bungalow. Later, the Carters moved to 833 West Seventh Street in town, where they were known for their spectacular outdoor Christmas tree.

Five teams of Percherons (above) are displayed outside the main barn. The local newspaper reported that they were the finest draft horses ever brought into the South. In November 1917, Clint Wharton informed R.J. Reynolds, "At Reynolda, we have bread [sic] all of our mares to Mr. Anderson's percheron horse, but some of our mares have refused him the past two periods, so I hope some of them are now safe in foal." In late afternoon, children gathered at the trough (below) to watch the Percherons come in from the fields to be watered. Nadeina Gibson, the electrician's daughter, described them as those "huge, big-hipped things that pulled the farm wagons." The trough also marked the spot where farmworkers waited to receive their orders in the morning and their pay on Saturday.

The structure on the near side of the cattle shed (above) was Robert Conrad's garage and his maid's room and bath. The cattle shed housed pedigreed Jersey bulls, which R.J. Reynolds introduced into the region in response to an appeal from agricultural associations to upgrade local livestock. Thomas Guy Monroe, the first herdsman, was asked to accompany R.J. Reynolds to Lexington, Kentucky, to help select the champion bulls. His son saw a letter describing the trip in which Monroe expressed his excitement over the opportunity, but he was more excited when R.J. offered him an Old Fashioned, his first mixed drink. He confessed that he liked it better than the swig of white lightning he had once before. Smith Reynolds (below) displays Xenias Rower Jr. while Clint Wharton's son Albert looks on.

When Thomas Guy Monroe came to work at Reynolda in 1914, a silo was considered a new development, which provided food for cows in winter. The silo (above) was packed from the top with corn stalks, legumes, and molasses. Heat and lack of air prevented the growth of bacteria, so when the silage was removed from the bottom, it was moist and digestible. The photograph below, taken from the walkway between the cow barn and the milk rooms, shows two doors on the right opening into the electric refrigerator plant, which was revolutionary in 1913 when it was installed. Most dairies depended on ice to keep milk cool, but as it melted the temperature rose, causing the milk to spoil. Refrigeration guaranteed an even temperature—a major factor in ensuring the safety of milk.

This view shows the group of barns with its silos, ventilators, and rooftops designed to create a beautiful effect from the pasture below. The lower floor of the gambrel-roofed building on the right served as a service station equipped with a gas pump as well as pits and grates for repairing automobiles. Since in the early years there were no commercial automobile repair shops in the area, it was necessary for Reynolda to maintain its own service station (below). In 1912, Katharine Reynolds gave Charles Barton Keen these specifications: the service station "should have a pit and an arrangement for lifting the tops off of cars and raising them to the roof for winter storage." At a time when the automobile was replacing the horse and carriage, this letter provides a valuable list of family vehicles reflecting this change: "It also should have a carriage room," Katharine wrote, "for a Victoria, Landau, and Buggy, and garage for four cars." (Above, TS; below, SH.)

This photograph shows the milk processing barn on the left and the cow barn on the right. The white double doors in the masonry on the ground level opened into the laundry. Its proximity to the cow barn was essential since dairymen's uniforms and wiping cloths required daily washing. Extreme sanitary precautions such as these were the only known ways to reduce the spread of serious milk-borne diseases.

In the barn behind the dairyman, the Jerseys were milked by machines, which were experimental when they were installed in 1916. Katharine Reynolds told a reporter for the local press that she selected Jerseys for "quality rather than quantity." She was referring to the fact that although Jerseys did not give a large amount of milk, the milk was high in butterfat, which, contrary to modern nutrition, was thought to be essential for good health.

The small white building in the center is the smokehouse, where hams and bacon were cured over hickory fires. Each autumn about 15 lean Tamworth hogs were slaughtered and brought to the area between the heating plant and the creek to be scraped and hung up for cleaning. These were considered festive occasions at which children were given bladders to blow up like balloons.

According to a story in the local newspaper, R.J. Reynolds chose Tamworths as the type of hogs raised at Reynolda. He had wanted to find "a breed with meat as sweet as that of the long-nosed piney woods rooters" that he had hunted in Georgia. He learned that the closest domestic hogs were Tamworths. Their reputation spread, and Forsyth County became known as "the Tamworth Capital of the South."

92

Alfred Drage Sr., who worked in the greenhouses as a team with his father, occupied the three-room frame cottage (above) with his wife, Marie, who stands on the porch with her son Al. Years later, he gave a description of a boy's life at Reynolda: "We had the run of the place. When they were hauling in the corn, they let us ride on top of the horses. We had access to the tennis courts; we swam in the pool behind the house. Just about anything we wanted to do." The Drages and three unidentified people (below) stand in front of their 1920 Dodge touring car. The photograph below shows Alfred standing on the running board with Marie, wearing the dark dress in front of him, and three unidentified people beside a 1920 Dodge Touring Car. (Both, AD.)

According to switchboard operator Elizabeth Wade, "Didn't anybody drive Miss Katharine but Cleve." She was referring to Cleveland Williams, Katharine Reynolds's personal chauffeur, who lived in a five-room cottage with his wife, Minnie Belle, their two sons, and his sister-in-law, Almeta Easley, who worked as a seamstress at the bungalow. His cottage (above) was located diagonally across from the heating plant. Wearing his tan summer chauffeur's uniform, Cleve (below) joins Smith and Nancy Reynolds in a game of croquet at the front of the bungalow. He wore Johnny Bulls, which caught the attention of Harvey Miller, a boy from Five Row. They were fashionable shoes, bought one size too large so that the toes would turn up.

By constructing the heating plant at the north end of the village (right), neither the 125-foot-tall smokestack nor the large piles of coal to fuel the furnaces detracted from the residential appearance of the estate. Moreover, by giving it a white, arcaded facade and keeping it low to the ground, Charles Barton Keen brought the utilitarian structure into harmony with the rest of the village. The map (below) shows the tunnels that carried utilities underground from the heating plant to the bungalow and to buildings on both sides of Reynolda Road. They provided endless fascination for children on the estate. Robert Conrad Jr. recalled, "I knew all the tunnels and where the manholes were. I'd park my bicycle in a bush, pull up the manhole cover, zip down, and come out at the heating plant."

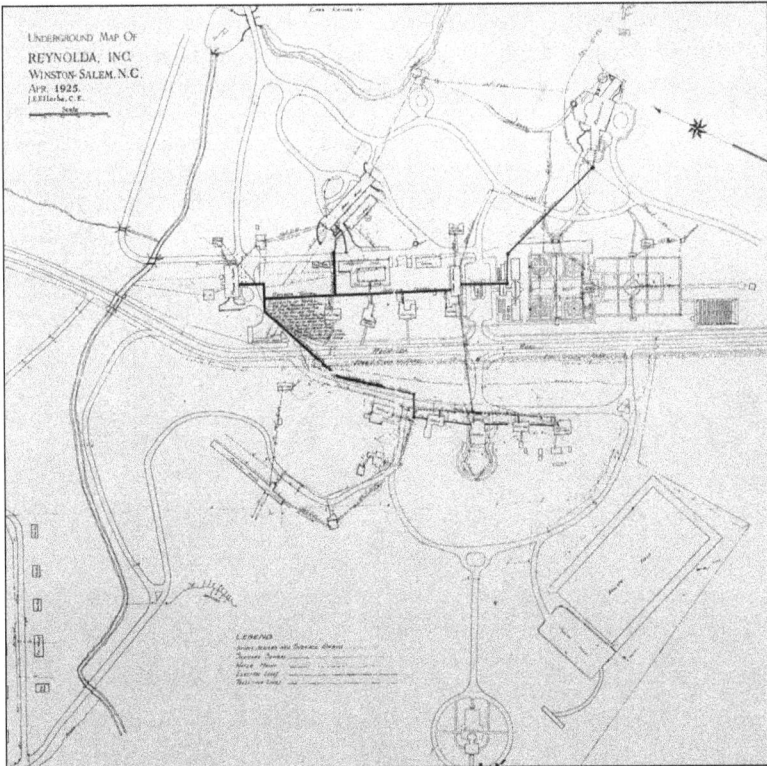

The blacksmith shop above was located on Reynolda Road, where it was accessible not only to estate vehicles but also to passersby. Considering the fact that horses and mules were the principal power source for building, landscaping, and maintaining the estate, the blacksmith who fitted them with iron shoes was crucial to its operations. From left to right, the snapshot below shows Clint Wharton on his horse; Smith Reynolds on a pony in front of Nancy Reynolds; Sallie Hayes, a French teacher at Reynolda School; and Carolyn "Sister" Wharton, Clint's daughter. When Nancy was attending high school, riding around the lake road was a daily event. Her mother had been an excellent horsewoman. She was often seen riding around the estate on Kentucky Belle, the finest saddle horse in the stables.

Seven

VILLAGE WEST OF REYNOLDA ROAD

In this 1927 aerial view of the village's west side, Reynolda Road extends at a diagonal on the right. Between it and the secondary road, a spring-fed brook runs through an area that Katharine Reynolds described as a "small natural park." A group of tiny white boxes below the circular walk marking the church amphitheater is the apiary that produced the tasty Reynolda honey.

A monumental rock water fountain stood between the entrance piers on the west side of Reynolda Road. The rocks, which originated as volcanic fragments of diabase dikes, were discovered during the excavation of the lake bed and used for masonry throughout the village. Prized for their rustic quality, they replaced commercial stone in the construction of walls, foundations, and chimneys.

Whoever persuaded Katharine Reynolds to pose next to the rock water fountain rendered a service to posterity, since informal photographs of her are rare. She had the public fountain built at the entrance to the village to provide passersby and their livestock with pure, safe water from the artesian well. In an era when waterborne diseases ran rampant, it presented a way to extend Reynolda's benefits.

The above detail of a 1916 panorama taken from Reynolda Road looks down the entrance drive toward Reynolda Presbyterian Church. From left to right are the farm superintendent's cottage, electrician's (later plumber's) cottage, and on the other side of the church, a cottage that was later moved up the hill to make room for the manse. The Thomas Sears planting plan below, with the rock water fountain drawn in at the bottom, shows the same road bordered by dense shrubs curling up from the brook, the banks of which were to be planted with Virginia sweetspire, pussy willow, and wild elder. Using these plants—which were associated with woods and bogs—rather than garden varieties was a new idea in landscape design and suggests that Katharine Reynolds encouraged progressive ideas in landscaping as well as in the development of her dairy and school.

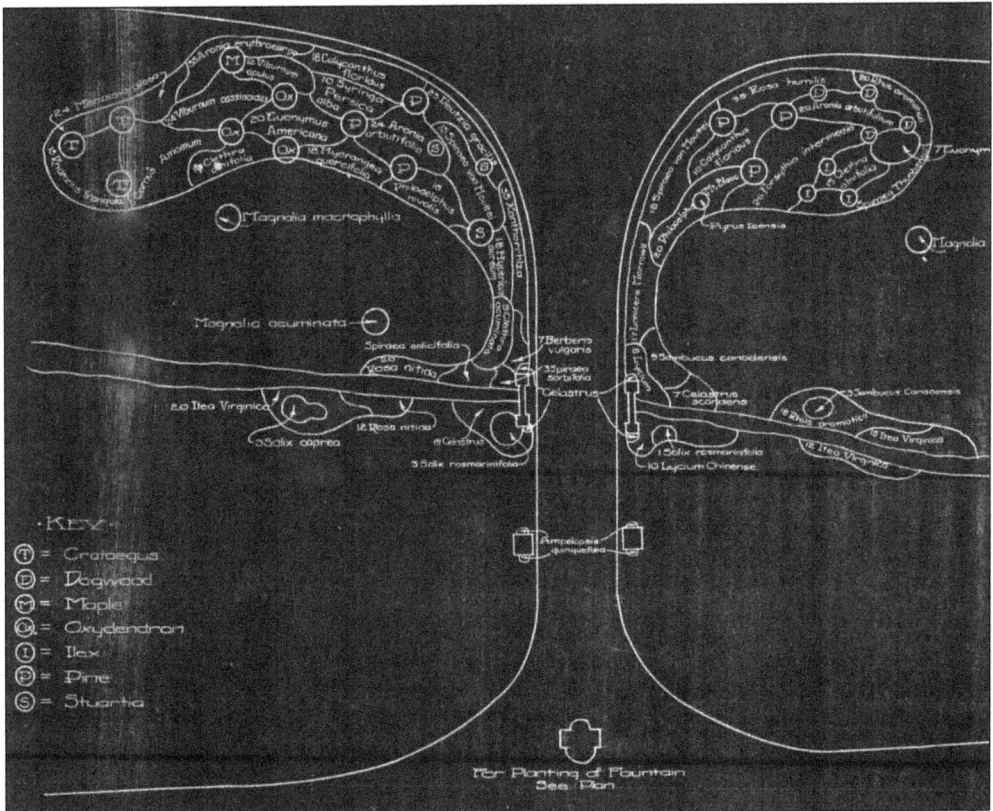

In 1912, Katharine Reynolds and other members of the First Presbyterian Church in town established a mission Sunday school at the Wachovia Arbor School House (above), located near the corner of Arbor and Reynolda Roads. Its purpose was to attract enough members to justify building a church at Reynolda. Dr. Neal Anderson, the minister, gave his approval, and he was said to follow the project "with affectionate interest." On November 28, 1915, he presided over the dedication of the completed church (below). Although it had just 32 members at the time, Katharine did not rest until the pews were full. She trudged over muddy roads to outlying farms, inviting families to her church. Her deepest concern, however, was that her husband had not joined. Finally, on July 5, 1917, she wrote to Anderson, "My happiness is complete. Mr. Reynolds joined the church this morning."

Few ministers could take their family for a Sunday drive in a royal blue Cadillac 30 (above), which came on the market in 1909, one year after Dr. Neal Anderson began his ministry at the First Presbyterian Church. Katharine Reynolds and her children attended his church before they moved their membership to the Reynolda Presbyterian Church (below). Although he was not a churchman, R.J. Reynolds took an interest in Anderson, a bright young Princeton graduate. When Anderson's daughter brought this photograph to the Reynolda archives, she told the following story: "Mr. Reynolds had asked her father to go for a ride with him in his wife's new Cadillac 30. He was interested in the minister's reaction to the automobile. Anderson must have been enthusiastic, since a week later, a Cadillac 30 appeared in his drive. It was a present from R.J. Reynolds."

In the portrait of a Sunday school class seen above, the girl in a hat on the right at the end of the second row is Mary Reynolds. The woman in the broad-brimmed hat in the last row is believed to be her mother, Katharine Reynolds, who frequently taught classes. She was remembered for giving gold stars to stick on each memorized page of the catechism. Al Drage Jr. recalled that when he recited the entire catechism, she gave him a Bible and a $5 gold piece. Her niece received a bicycle. The women seen below standing outside the church are also members of a Sunday school class. The only one who has been identified is Lizzie Thompson, the Reynolds children's nurse, at the far right.

Soon after the church was completed, the congregation asked Katharine Reynolds to build the "outdoor auditorium" (above) where services could be held in the fresh air. She turned to Thomas Sears, who came up with an ingenious solution. He flattened the hill behind the church into a round, sunken lawn and encircled it with a walk, embankment, and a hedge of Italian cypress. On June 15, 1918, Charles Kent and Senah Critz, R.J. Reynolds's niece, were married there in front of the west facade of the church (below). With twin half-timbered gables flanking stained-glass windows by the Philadelphia firm of Nichola D'Ascenzo, the west facade seems to have been designed with ceremonies such as this in mind. Sunday services and school pageants were also held there.

On November 10, 1912, Katharine Reynolds boasted in a letter to a friend, "The farm is flourishing now. I am acting superintendent." The remark coincided with the departure of civil engineer R.E. Snowden, who had overseen the early construction phase of the estate. She now looked for a man knowledgeable in up-to-date agricultural practices. By 1915, the man seen at left—A. Clinton Wharton, a graduate in scientific agriculture from North Carolina A&M College—was on the payroll and moving into the newly completed cottage above. His degree qualified him to introduce farmers in the region to scientific methods of agriculture. In 1919, when J. Edward Johnston was hired as the Reynolda School principal, he boarded with the Whartons. His teachers lived nearby in the manse. Sallie Hayes, the French teacher, poses with Clint after a horseback ride (left).

Local architect Willard C. Northup designed the electrician's cottage (above) with a lattice-enclosed front porch and built-in settles, evoking the homespun character of an English country cottage. Situated between the superintendent's cottage and the Reynolda Presbyterian Church, it was built for Robert A. Gibson, the electrician. After living for six years in this cottage, the Gibsons were moved into the Northup cottage below, which was relocated up the hill behind the church. A comparison of the two cottages reveals that the Gibsons were upgraded from a five-room to seven-room house, thereby improving their living standards considerably. Daughter Nadeina (below) recalled occasional visits from Katharine Reynolds, whom she found "very down to earth." One morning, Mrs. Reynolds dropped in when Nadeina's mother was cooking, and "she sat at the kitchen table and ate green beans and biscuits."

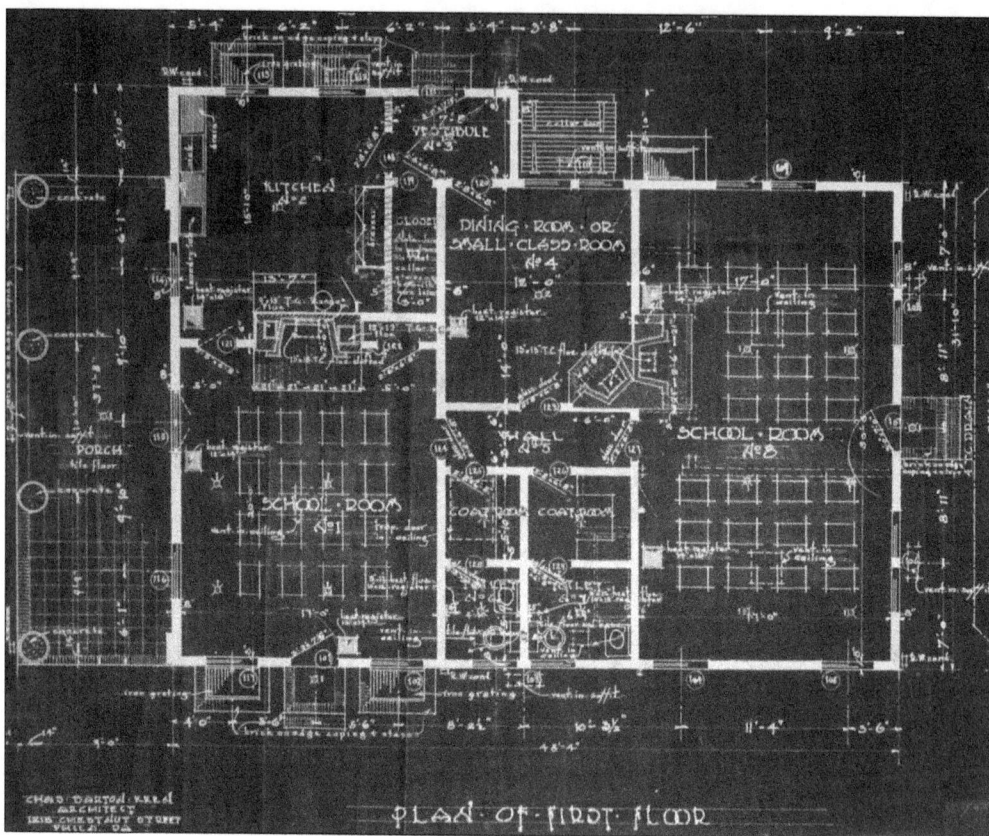

PLAN·OF·FIRST·FLOOR

The cottage seen below stands on the corner across from the manse. Its low roofline, recessed porch, and squat columns are typical bungalow features. Since only the main residence was allowed to claim this designation, it was invariably described as a cottage. In fact, from 1918 to 1921, it served as the lower schoolhouse. Dated August 8, 1918, Charles Barton Keen's blueprint for a "Cottage and Temporary School House" (above), shows that the house had two schoolrooms, one of which could be partitioned into two. One room contained 16 desks, and the other contained 25 desks. The school opened in 1918 under the direction of Minnie Morrison with about 20 students in grades one through three. Nadeina Gibson, who lived next door, recalled that her classroom was in the kitchen, and that one room was devoted entirely to crafts.

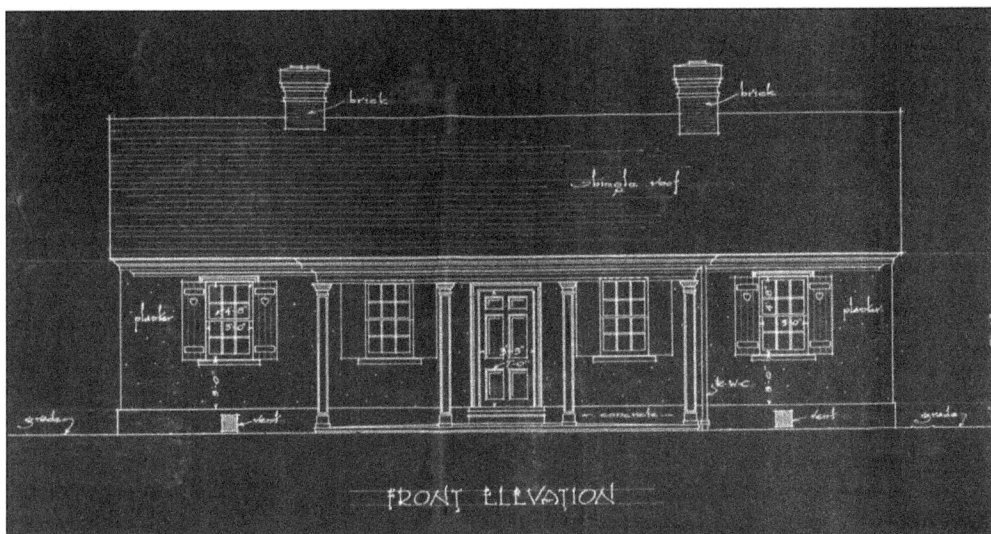

FRONT ELEVATION

A front elevation of this cottage (above), which stood on a hill overlooking Reynolda Road opposite the blacksmith shop, identifies Charles Barton Keen as its architect. With the exception of the bungalow, only a smattering of Keen's plans has survived. This one is dated February 8, 1916. The best-known occupants of this cottage during Katharine Reynolds's lifetime were James Drage and his Irish wife, whose brogue delighted the neighbors. He was hired to manage the greenhouses along with his son Alfred. Trained in England, James knew the Latin names of nearly every plant. He had worked for a time in South Africa before he came to Wilmington, Delaware, where he was employed at one of the du Pont estates. He and his son started work at Reynolda in 1921 and left some time after Katharine's death in 1924. Considering the short time they stayed, they made quite an impact.

Located next to the church, the 10-room manse (above) was the second-largest house at Reynolda. In 1921, after it was completed, the teachers at Reynolda School occupied it. After the school closed, Katharine Reynolds used her persuasive skills to lure Dr. D. Clay Lilly (left) away from his parish in Lexington, Kentucky, to serve as minister at the Reynolda Presbyterian Church. During the years that he was at the First Presbyterian Church in Winston-Salem, he had presided over her wedding to R.J. Reynolds, and in 1918, he officiated at R.J.'s funeral. The special place that he held as her spiritual advisor was demonstrated again in 1921, when he agreed to officiate at her marriage to J. Edward Johnston. (Left, FP.)

As occupants of the manse, Dr. D. Clay Lilly and his family enjoyed its large, walled garden designed by Thomas Sears. This view shows a deep perennial border running along a stucco wall with brick coping. At the corner, the wall curves outward to accommodate a semicircular bench backed by a cluster of young cedars. The open space in the background later became the site of the Katharine Smith Johnston Memorial building. (TS.)

This view shows a flagstone walk extending along the south side of the manse, leading to the garden in the rear. A boxwood hedge runs along the outside, and a floral border softens both edges. Over time, the ivy, which has already begun to climb in this photograph, covered the entire wall, and the lack of shutters allowed it to surround the window casing. (TS.)

The poultry house and runs (above) were located on the hill behind the Gibson's second cottage. They were built large enough to fulfill Katharine Reynolds's ambition to establish a business selling guinea hens to "hotels and cafés of the North and East." News of her intentions had reached Thomas Settle, an attorney at law from Asheville, who wrote, "I see from the papers that you have gone into the poultry raising business on the largest scale ever attempted in this section." But by then, the war had curtailed her ambitions. She answered, "I have come down to just two kinds, the white leghorns for laying and the Plymouth Rocks for broilers. . . . It is our intention to stick to the two above-mentioned breeds, as our object, until the war is over, is to raise meat rather than fine feathers." Some of the white leghorns are shown in the photograph below.

Eight

FIVE ROW

Mamie and Henry Miller, pictured with granddaughters Nancy Sue (left) and Brenda, moved to Five Row in 1922. Katharine Reynolds built the community of Five Row for African American farmworkers employed at Reynolda and their families. Henry drove a mule team and did jobs such as hauling coal to the heating plant, mowing the golf course, and plowing fields. He made $18 a week, which he considered a good wage. The Millers' son Harvey attended the Five Row School and later became majordomo for Katharine Reynolds's daughter, Mary Babcock. (HM.)

This 1927 aerial view shows the turnoff from Reynolda Road to Five Row, which was built along Silas Creek. Today, this view would show the intersection of Reynolda Road and Silas Creek Parkway, near the entrance to Wake Forest University. The heating plant is visible in the middle right, and the blue granite quarry, which supplied gravel for construction materials, is visible in the lower section. With the exception of the pump house at the outdoor swimming pool, the granite was not used for masonry. Its value lay in gravel for paving roads, mixing concrete, and, in its finest form, for paths in the vegetable garden. Al Drage Jr. lived in a house close enough to the quarry to recall, "When they got ready to blast, they sounded the whistle from the steam plant, and everybody ran indoors. We had rocks flying over our house and everything else."

The white cluster of houses in the upper left corner of the detail above from a 1927 aerial view shows the location of Five Row in relation to the rest of the estate. The 1925 map below shows Five Row as two rows of houses flanking an unpaved road, which runs parallel to Silas Creek. The first houses in Five Row date from 1916 and were arranged in two rows of five (with one added later), a layout that gave the community its name. The road running through the village connects on the east to Reynolda Road and on the west to another unpaved road, which after 1923 led up a hill to the polo fields.

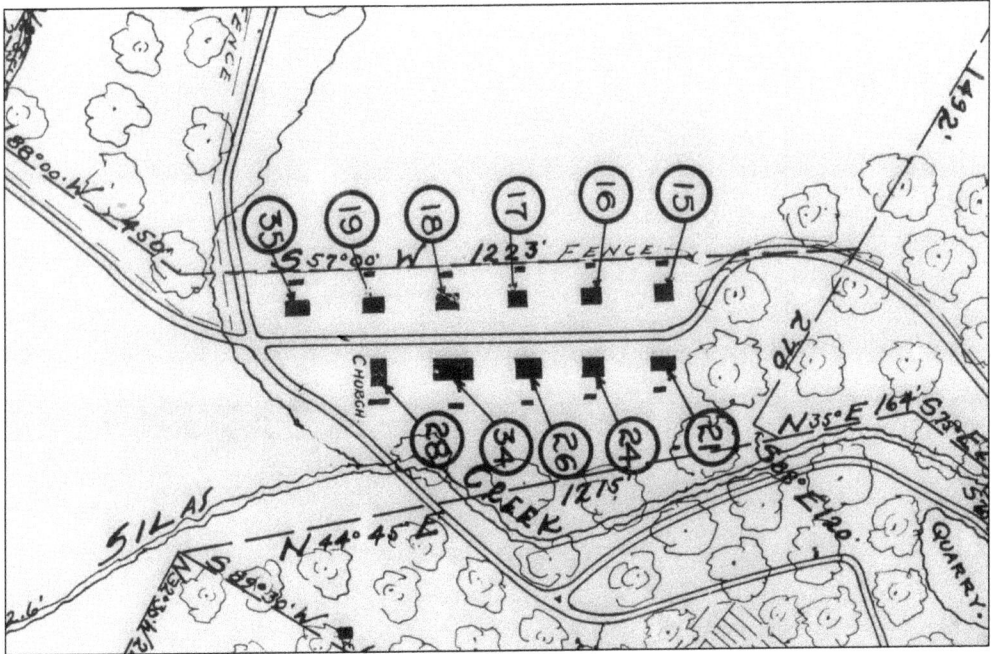

Thomas Warren stands outside the Five Row School (left), which opened with only six students in 1918, the same year that Katharine Reynolds started a lower school for white children in the main village. She must have ordered furniture and supplies in bulk; Harvey Miller, a student, remembers that the desks and textbooks were the same in both schools. Classes were held in two rooms, which were combined for church services on Sundays. Students studied history, geography, spelling, grammar, and arithmetic. They read Washington Irving's "Rip Van Winkle," and they memorized Abraham Lincoln's "Gettysburg Address." Painting, drawing, and music—subjects that were not available in public schools at this time—were also offered. The snapshot below shows a side view of the schoolhouse.

When Katharine Reynolds asked Lovey Eaton (right) to teach at the school that she was starting at Five Row, Lovey was working as Katharine's maid. She had taken courses in teacher training and from all accounts was an excellent teacher and a hard taskmaster. Over time, the number of students grew from six to more than 34. The two women standing in the back row in the photograph below are Mrs. Kearns, a teacher, and Anna Webster, the second principal. The young man in light-colored trousers standing at the left is Harvey Miller, who provided a number of oral histories recounting life at Five Row. Because the school year ran for eight months instead of the customary six, and because it offered art and music, it drew children from a range of economic backgrounds. In addition, the Five Row School outlasted the Reynolda School by 20 years.

Flora Pledger and Lillie Hamlin, early residents of Five Row, stand outside the schoolyard (above). A volleyball net and an outhouse are visible in the background. Harvey Miller described the yard as a large area with "a volleyball court, basketball, croquet, and horseshoes." Flora's husband worked as a laborer, and Lillie's drove a mule team (below). The wives raised children and took part-time jobs, especially at hog-killing time. According to Flora, Five Row residents preferred hogs that gave large quantities of lard to the lean Tamworths raised at Reynolda. "The men took it for fun," she explained, "to see which one could raise the biggest hogs. And you never seen such hogs in your life. Oh, we raised one 550 pounds. And lard! I had three cans about *that big*, full of lard."

The photograph at right shows five-year-old Harvey Miller at about the time his family moved from town to Five Row. As a teenager, he took on various jobs at Reynolda: washing cars for Buck Wharton, babysitting for Robert Conrad, and hauling firewood for Mattie Duffy, the cook at the bungalow. He also caddied for golfers on the Reynolda course and became a lifelong golfer himself. He was hired as butler for Katharine and R.J. Reynolds's daughter, Mary Babcock, and with the exception of his service in the army during World War II, he worked for the family his entire life. He and his wife, Rosalie Eaton (below), are photographed at Five Row with a cow looking on. Since the women are wearing hats and white dresses, the snapshot was undoubtedly taken after church. (Both, HM.)

Although taken in the 1950s, these are the only photographs that show the dirt road running through Five Row. Behind Ida Lash and her son Wayne (left), a telephone pole is visible, indicating that by the 1950s, utilities had arrived. Samuel Stimpson (below), who had a lifelong career in the armed forces, is standing beside a 1940 Plymouth. In the background, three Five Row houses are visible. Each one had a front yard defined by a privet hedge and a vegetable garden in the rear. In the early days, like most farmhouses, they did not have indoor plumbing, but they did have safe drinking water. When the village was built, pipes were laid all the way from the artesian well on the golf course to Five Row. In 1961, Five Row was demolished to make way for Silas Creek Parkway. (Both, EL.)

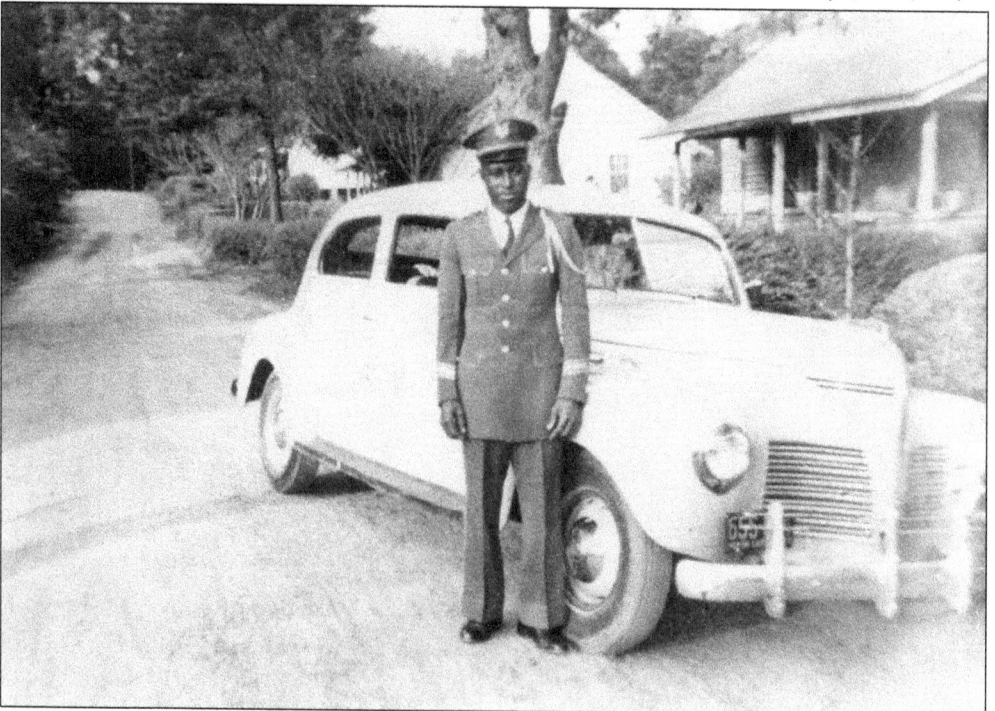

Nine

GARDEN PARTIES, POLO, AND MEMORIALS

Mary (left) and Nancy, 12 and 11 years old, pose in their fashionable Boué Soeurs dresses, which they wore as flower girls at their mother's wedding to J. Edward Johnston on June 11, 1921. Their younger brother Smith served as ring bearer. Only family members and close friends attended the ceremony. Mary entered in her diary, "We are trying to keep it quiet, but about the whole town knows about it."

Standing outside the lake porch, Mario Chamlee points toward the setting for his recital on June 8, 1921. Katharine Reynolds, an avid music lover, had invited the sensational new tenor from the Metropolitan Opera to give an outdoor performance for 500 guests. Few knew the real reason for the celebration until three days later, when they opened the newspapers and read the announcement of her marriage to J. Edward Johnston.

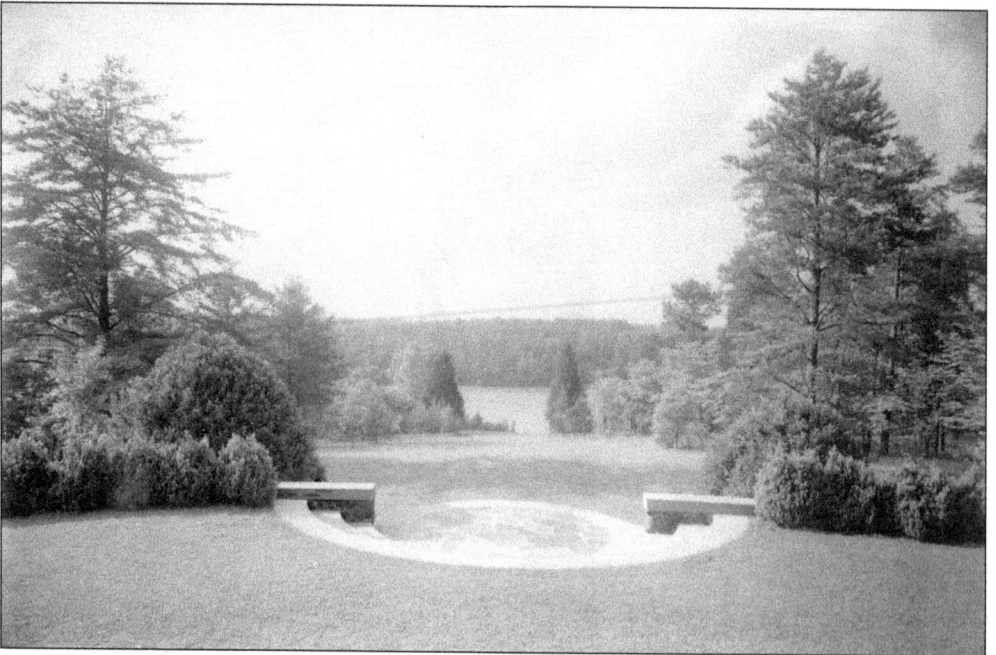

Tucked into the center of the grass terrace off the lake porch, two sets of curved steps—one concave and the other convex—enclose a round platform, which became the stage for the Mario Chamlee recital. It was described in the local newspaper as the most "brilliant social event [that] had ever been given in the Twin-City."

At 28, the groom was considerably younger than the bride, who was 41 at the time of their marriage. A native of Florence, South Carolina, J. Edward Johnston (right) graduated from Davidson College in 1914. He taught for a time before he enlisted in the US Army. During World War I, he served as a lieutenant with the 1st Division of the 5th Field Artillery Battalion in France. After his discharge, he applied for the position of principal of Reynolda School, which was expanding through the seventh grade. Toward the end of his first year at the school, he and Katharine (below), who had been a widow for nearly two years, fell in love. Neither Katharine nor Edward took lightly the discrepancies in their age and income. Letters indicate that they sought advice from trusted advisors before they made the decision to marry.

On the evening of June 11, 1921, Katharine Reynolds was married to J. Edward Johnston in front of the fireplace in the reception hall at Reynolda. Here she is photographed in her white satin wedding dress trimmed with real pearls and a train of Brussels lace. Ethel Brock, one of the teachers, believed the romance started in March 1920, when both were on a trip with a group of consultants to visit high schools in preparation for building an auditorium in memory of R.J. Reynolds. When Katharine informed her parents of her engagement, she wrote, "I have worked and planned for the happiness of others, but now I am working and planning for my own." On their honeymoon, the couple must have been pleased when they received a letter from Bum, the governess, reporting that Nancy had confessed: "I am so happy; it is wonderful to have a father again."

The lovely dress and hat worn by Ruth Smith, Katharine Reynolds's sister (right), added to the charm of the setting seen below for the afternoon garden party, held on July 6, 1923. Katharine and J. Edward Johnston invited 1,200 guests to meet Charles Barton Keen, architect, Dr. D. Clay Lilly, minister, and their wives. US Bureau of Internal Revenue commissioner David Hunt Blair and his wife were also included in the receiving line. Punch was served from bowls made of huge chunks of ice embedded with flowers. As evening approached, guests dined under the light of Japanese lanterns strung from the cryptomeria trees and danced to Paul Whiteman's Romance of Rhythm Band.

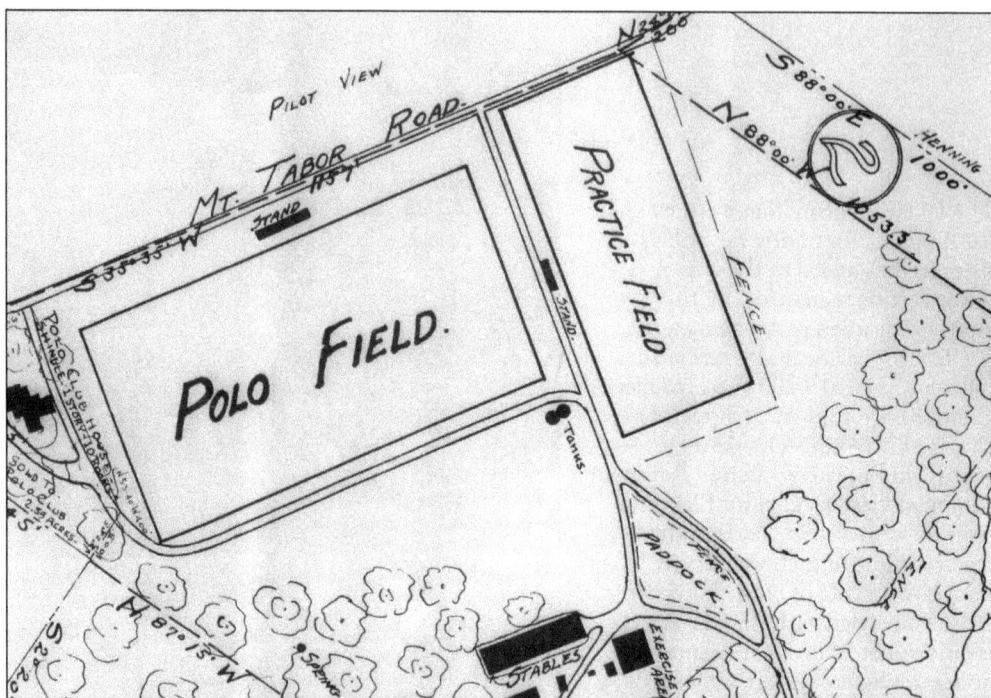

POLO
This Afternoon
At 5 O'Clock
Reynolda Polo Field
EXHIBITION GAME
OF 5 CHUKKARS
The Public is Cordially Invited
Admission 50 Cents

In 1923, J. Edward Johnston became a major force in organizing a polo team for Winston-Salem. The sport became so popular that Katharine purchased the Henning property north of Reynolda, seen above. There, two regulation fields—one for practice and the other for tournament games—were built. Mount Tabor Road (now Polo Road) marked the northern boundary of the polo fields, which are occupied today by Speas Elementary School. The *Winston-Salem Journal* published the advertisement (left) for an exhibition game.

Members of the Winston-Salem polo team are shown here lined up for a photograph. From left to right are A.C. Wharton, Carl Ogburn, polo club manager W.V. Slocock, James G. Hanes, Benjamin F. Bernard, Watt Martin, Thurmond Chatham, J. Edward Johnston, and Fred M. Hanes. The club hired a polo professional to select the ponies, coach the players, and—when he was not playing—act as referee.

This photograph shows automobiles parked along the roped-off polo field at Reynolda. Polo attracted large crowds to the end of the 1920s, but it was a costly sport and did not survive the Great Depression. The name Polo Road has been retained as one of the few reminders of the early attraction to this area.

Most likely taken at one of the polo matches, this snapshot shows Katharine Reynolds (above left) as most people saw her—not a beauty, but a warm, likable, and intelligent woman. Between her and mother-in-law Lola Johnston stands Ben Bernard, a polo player who was employed as Katharine's secretary. The house Katharine built for Lola on Reynolda Road (below) was part of a development in the Kent Road area, which Thomas Sears was laying out and landscaping. In July 1923, Katharine wrote to her daughter Mary, who was visiting Atlantic City with Lola, her new grandmother, "Mr. Sears was here yesterday, and we spent time going over the new development plans. Tell grandmother her lot is being laid off and is going to be lovely."

Katharine died on May 23, 1924, just three days after giving birth to J. Edward Johnston Jr., the boy posing with his father in the photograph at right. Doctors had warned her that because of her weak heart, pregnancy was dangerous. Nonetheless, believing in the importance of families, she became pregnant, hoping to survive. Her death left her four children by R.J. Reynolds orphans. Her will appointed J. Edward Johnston and her brother-in-law William N. Reynolds as guardians. Edward had the Katharine Smith Johnston Monument (below) built in her memory.

Visit us at
arcadiapublishing.com

....

www.ingramcontent.com/pod-product-compliance
Lightning Source LLC
Chambersburg PA
CBHW050544110426
42813CB00008B/2255